Engaging Young Children

Engaging Young Children

A Nurturing Pedagogy

**Nóirín Hayes
and Margaret Kernan**

GILL & MACMILLAN

Gill & Macmillan Ltd
Hume Avenue
Park West
Dublin 12
with associated companies throughout the world
www.gillmacmillan.ie

978 07171 4457 0

Index compiled by Cover to Cover
Print origination in Ireland by Carole Lynch

The paper used in this book is made from the wood pulp
of managed forests. For every tree felled, at least one tree
is planted, thereby renewing natural resources.

A CIP catalogue record for this book is available
from the British Library.

Contents

Foreword

Engaging Young Children is an exciting landmark in the development of pedagogy for young children in early childhood education and care settings. The book reflects on rapid worldwide changes in the lives of parents and young children. Since the 1970s there have been heated discussions about the working mother in most Western countries. Often the women's movement has been seen to stand for mothers' interests and the pedagogues and psychologists for children's – as if the two were opposed (Singer, 1998). But since the end of the twentieth century, new attitudes, theoretical approaches and practices have become dominant. Early childhood services for young children are generally accepted, not only because parents have to work outside the home but also because of their pedagogical value. How to provide quality childcare and education for young children has become the main question. *Engaging Young Children* takes up that challenge. The authors offer a clear overview of the historical developments of early childhood education policy and theoretical thinking in Ireland within an international context. Additionally, new insights are provided with respect to common theoretical concepts of child development. The book contributes to the construction of new theoretical frameworks that relate to daily practices of quality childcare in Ireland and other Western countries.

The book is rich and challenging and cannot be summarised easily. But a few key messages stand out. Firstly, the *child is an active agent* in his or her development. The concept of the active child pervades the book and is operationalised in examples of inspiring pedagogical practices. Teachers listen to children and are able to 'tune into' their interests. They provide opportunities for positive interactions between children and their environment that are both safe and risk rich. An active, learning child cannot explore the world without occasionally having grazes and bruises on his or her knees. The concept of the active child is based on the work of Piaget, Vygotsky and recent constructivist approaches to child development. The concept also relates to empirical studies of young children's play and learning [**ref to come**] and social lives in child-care groups (Singer & De Haan, 2007). Since young children learn and live with peers in childcare groups, researchers, teachers and adults have become aware of infants' and toddlers' skills in com-municating and co-constructing shared meanings. Ideas about the egocentrism of young children have been changed radically because of observations in childcare settings.

The second key concept that is central to the book is that of *'nurturing pedagogy'*. Active learning children need *active adults* who create learning environments that are rich in both language and content. Teachers are the architects of an emerging curriculum. They observe the children, talk with them and engage in shared exploration of the world. They take care of balance between safety and challenge; between nurture and education; between play and responsibilities of the children; between freedom and rules.Teachers also organise a variety of play experiences, including creative activ-ities, music, physical activities, early mathematics, language and reading. In the view of the authors of *Engaging Young Children*, adults play a critical role in supporting young children's learning.

The authors enrich the concept of nurturing pedagogy by dis-cussing the historical roots. They go back to pioneers of early child-hood education such as Margaret McMillan and show how the idea of nurturing pedagogy builds on 150 years of pedagogical thinking. Every generation critically discusses the heritage of earlier generations and revises central concepts to adapt to the changing social contexts and pedagogical ideals. The book acknowledges the tradition and attainments of earlier generations. It also highlights that bringing up children is a social endeavour. This is the third key concept I want to point at. Every chapter communicates that learning and teaching are the result of *interactions and relationships*. Children learn by interacting with peers, adults and their environment. Their sense of security is dependent on a sense of belonging to the group. Children need warm relationships with their teachers and peers and between their parents and teachers. In good-quality childcare settings, adults and children form a community of learners. Teachers learn from each other and the children on a daily basis, and they critically adapt the content and the processes to the needs and interests of the children. Therefore, the development of pedagogy for young children is an ongoing process, historically and on the level of daily practice. *Engaging Young Children* is an inspiring and challenging landmark within this rapidly changing world of early childhood education and care.

Dr Elly Singer

Singer, E. *Child Care and the Psychology of Development*, (London/New York: Routledge 1992).

Singer, E. & de Haan, D. *The Social Lives of Young Children: Play, Conflict and Moral Learning in Day-care Groups* (Amsterdam: B.V. Uitgeverij SWP 2007).

Acknowledgments

The ideas presented in this book go back a long way and we owe a great deal to our friends and colleagues, nationally and internationally, who have challenged our thinking, encouraged our work and contributed to its refinement. In particular we would like to acknowledge the interest and support of our colleagues at the Dublin Institute of Technology. The book derives in part from doctoral research and we are grateful to all who provided advice and guidance, in particular the children, parents and early years practitioners who make up the wider context from which the book has emerged. In their work on developing a National Framework for Early Learning, the National Council for Curriculum and Assessment, especially Arlene Foster, provided a valuable space to both authors for testing ideas with a wider population of academics, practitioners and policymakers. Useful discussions were also had with staff and partners of the Bernard van Leer Foundation, particularly in relation to respect for diversity.

Our contacts in Gill & Macmillan deserve special mention. Marion O'Brien and Emma Farrell were always there in the background, gently ensuring that deadlines were met.

As ever, a work such as this depends on the patience and goodwill of our families who have lived with this work, one way or another, over many years.

To everyone – thank you. All errors, woolly thinking and omissions are ours and ours alone.

Chapter one

Engaging Young Children

INTRODUCTION

There have been significant changes in the field of early childhood education and care in Ireland over the last decade. Responding to the increasing demands for provision arising from the growing participation of women in the workforce and the rise in immigration, there has been unprecedented investment in the expansion of places and the infrastructure to manage such developments. To a somewhat lesser extent there has been investment in supports for services to enhance the quality and sustainability of provision. This can be seen in the various financial supports to parents, the publication of *Síolta – the National Quality Framework*, the development of a *National Framework for Early Learning* and the investment in a National Training Initiative. It is from within this context that the idea for this book emerged.

The book is about the theory and processes that inform daily practice with young children in early childhood education and care settings. It has been written at a time when, nationally and inter-nationally, there has been a rapid expansion of services and more young children are spending time in a range of settings such as preschools, infant classes, playgroups, day-care centres, crèches, nurseries and childminding settings. This development has been accompanied by a growing recognition of the importance of quality early childhood education experiences for all children in terms of lasting educational, developmental and social benefits, in addition to a view of access to quality early childhood education and care as a right for all children (Department of Health and Children, 2000; NESF, 2005; OECD, 2004).

The term 'pedagogy' is used throughout to capture the integrated processes of teaching and learning and the principles, theory, values and approaches that underpin daily work with young children in the range of early childhood education and care settings. Pedagogy encompasses the processes of children learning, whereby adults create learning opportunities and environments that engage, challenge and interest young children. It also focuses attention on the everyday learning that teachers of young children themselves engage in as they observe, reflect on and critically analyse the content and approach to their work with children, alone and with other adults. The book is therefore about relationships and interactions: between children, between adults and young children, between adults and their colleagues and parents of the children they work with, and between learners and the environments where learning takes place.

Why this book now?

The approach to the writing of this book, and its content, is located within the context of a number of current developments that are directly influencing daily work in early childhood education care settings. These developments include: (i) the professionalising of the early childhood education and care sector, encompassing the expansion of and provision of higher level training and the development of standards of good practice and ethics; (ii) a period of unprecedented social, cultural and technological change, including increased heterogeneity of societies; (iii) the almost universal ratification of the United Nations Convention on the Rights of the

Child, which is viewed by some as setting the scene for a twenty-first century focus on pedagogical work with children in the form of rights-based and social justice framework; and emerging from these (iv) the notion of early childhood education and care settings as sites of democratic practice whereby children and adults can participate collectively in interpreting experiences and shaping decisions affecting themselves (Moss, 2007); and (v) the centrality of the principles of social inclusion and respect for diversity in good quality early childhood education and care.

These global phenomena are slowly beginning to impact on services for young children worldwide. The particular focus in this book is how they are being interpreted and experienced in the national context of early childhood education and care in Ireland. In this sense, the book highlights the particularity of the experience of early childhood education and care in Ireland, drawing on its history, traditions, values, strengths and challenges. It also provides a critical review of current knowledge, which is located within an Irish perspective.

The importance of theory

The content of this book is based on the premise that the most effective early childhood practice is that which has a sound theoretical basis. Seven linked themes or key messages that are derived from research and theorising are emphasised throughout. These, it is proposed, provide a 'central thread' and ensure a coherent view of early childhood pedagogy which is meaningful at the beginning of the twenty-first century and which has applicability in a range of contexts.

The view of *young children as active agents in their own learning* is a recurring theme throughout. This concept is discussed both through a sociological and developmental psychological lens. Thus the tensions between the structuring and the agency in children's lives in terms of how they impact on their experiences of space and time in early childhood education and care settings are discussed, in addition to analysing the competing notions of development as structure versus development as process. Related to this is the second theme, which is *the dynamic, social and interactive nature of early learning*. Whilst the child is located at the heart of practice, the focus of discussion is placed equally on the child and the adult in interdependent relations as they engage in joint learning. Thus in the view of pedagogy presented here, much attention is paid to *the critical role of the adult* in supporting children's learning, thus representing the third theme. Extending this in a fourth theme, is the conceptualisation of *early childhood education and care as nurture*. The concept of nurture, proposed by early childhood pioneers such as Margaret McMillan, is revisited in the present text. Here it is reformulated to emphasise the educative nature of care and to place as central the critical and active role of the adult in effective, engaging and quality early education. The fifth theme emphasised is the *notion of content-, language- and risk-rich environments*. Children's interactions with the social and physical environments should be challenging and rich in both language and content and the onus is on the adult to provide such enabling environments. Viewing early childhood environments through an ecological lens is proposed as one means of creating and sustaining content- and risk-rich environments. The sixth theme stresses the *importance of play and playfulness as a pathway to learning*. As with other themes of analysis, we consider play from the perspectives of both the child and the adult, recognising the importance of the process of play to children, as well as the role of play as a window for the adult into the world of the sensing, active and playful child. The seventh and final theme concerns the *affective dimension of learning*. In this regard we prioritise *a sense of security and belonging* in early childhood education and care settings. This is the softer, less easy to measure dimension of learning. Importantly, however, it also allows attention to the consideration of valuable learning dispositions such as motivation, learner identity and confidence.

Approaches to the writing

Two key factors have underpinned the approach to the writing. Firstly, from the outset it was felt that an interdisciplinary approach would add richness to the analysis, offering the possibilities of new knowledge and understanding. Studies of early childhood from historical, psychological, educational, sociological, anthropological, geographical and related perspectives are drawn on in this book. The ensuing analysis has also been supported by the diverse backgrounds and experiences of the two authors within the field of early childhood education and care.

The second important factor guiding the writing process is the fact that it coincides with the publication of two major practice documents which have the potential to impact on early education practice in Ireland. These are, firstly, the *Síolta – The National Quality Framework* (CECDE, 2006) and *The Framework for Early Learning* (forthcoming), a national curriculum including practice guidelines for early education in Ireland which is being developed by the National Council for Curriculum and Assessment. Both these documents are derived from extensive consultation with practitioners and are informed by current research. It is hoped that this book, which is both practical and challenging, will support the reflection, analysis and interpretation required in the implementation of these guidelines. In this regard, reference is made to particular aspects of both documents wherever relevant.

How the book is organised

The book contains eight chapters. The introduction section of each chapter describes its focus and provides signposts for the reader to the particular areas of discussion and analysis to follow. Each chapter ends with a summary paragraph that offers a brief synthesis of the key messages contained in the chapter. This is accompanied by a 'points for reflection' section which is intended to stimulate personal reflection, discussion and debate.

Chapter 2 elaborates on the context of current developments in early childhood pedagogy in terms of its historical origins in Europe from the eighteenth century to the present day. It traces how ideas and theories emanating from so-called 'pioneers' of early childhood pedagogy, such as Froebel, Montessori and McMillan, were interpreted in Ireland. This chapter also analyses the current policy context in Ireland regarding early childhood education and care and considers the place of children, their interests and concerns, within such policy.

In Chapter 3, early childhood pedagogy is located within a broad multidisciplinary literature. Drawing on concepts, theoretical constructs and images of childhood from fields of study ranging from sociology of childhood to geography, as well as child development and developmental psychology, this chapter introduces new possibilities for conceptualising early childhood pedagogy.

In Chapters 4 to 7 the attention is placed firmly on the dynamics of children's learning, the contexts in which learning takes place and the roles and responsibilities of the adult. The relationship between development, learning and early childhood education is discussed in Chapter 4. This discussion is informed by a wide range of learning and development theory, some of which may already be familiar to the reader, such as the writings of Piaget, Vygotsky and Bronfenbrenner. However, some newer and less familiar ideas are also presented in this chapter. These serve to expand on the notions of: the active participation of the child in context; a view of development as a dynamic and discontinuous process; and positive learning dispositions.

Chapter 5 builds on the issues and concepts highlighted in Chapter 4 by exploring a range of understandings attached to the term 'curriculum' as applied in early childhood pedagogy. This chapter reviews the research that has evaluated the relative effectiveness of different models and approaches to early childhood curriculum. It also examines the values and principles that underpin a range of curricula currently in use in New Zealand, England,

United States, Italy, Scandinavia and Ireland, as well as those under-pinning the Framework for Early Learning being developed by the National Council for Curriculum and Assessment.

Chapter 6 places to the fore the importance of adults recognising their role as learners so they can effectively respond to individual children. The chapter begins with an overview of John Dewey's ideas on learning and development. This leads to the elaboration of the concept of a 'nurturing pedagogy', as a means by which curriculum may be realised in practice.

In Chapter 7 the interactive nature of learning is discussed with particular reference to children's interactions with the physical environments of early childhood education and care settings. This chapter considers the match between pedagogical vision and the design and organisation of space. Drawing on historical material, it also examines the points of continuity and change in designing spaces for young children. A number of concepts and perspectives that are becoming more commonplace in design in early childhood education and care are also highlighted and their applicability in everyday work with young children is discussed. Chapter 8 provides a synthesis of the book with particular reference to its applicability to current developments in policy, practice and training in Ireland.

In conclusion, and as noted above, our attention in this book is on the centrality of the child in the learning process as well as on the critical role of the adult in early childhood pedagogy. The term *early childhood education and care* is used throughout to describe the range of settings outside the family home where young children spend their time. The use of this term is in line with international convention, specifically the OECD (2000, 2006). The focus is on children from birth to the age of six. When referring to adults working with children in early childhood education and care settings, the terms *early years practitioner*, *teacher*, and *adult* are used interchangeably. This book is built upon the premise that all such adults are engaged in specialised and complex work, encompassing a wide range of roles and responsibilities which are underpinned by sound theoretical knowledge and expertise, ethical and safe practice, continuous reflection, critical review and learning and always within supportive environments.

The book aims to support undergraduate and postgraduate students of early childhood education and care, experienced and novice practitioners, trainers and teacher educators and other early childhood professionals, and to encourage critical dialogue about early childhood pedagogy. Theories, knowledge and ways of working, both old and new, require critical appraisal. We hope that readers will take up the challenge of identifying those that are most valuable and meaningful to the contexts in which they operate so that they can articulate their own positions on the ideas presented.

Chapter two

Early Childhood Education and Care Through a Socio-historical Lens

INTRODUCTION

Early childhood pedagogy is influenced by a number of interconnected factors, including dominant political discourses, economics and fundamental concerns such as understandings of childhood – regarding what children are or should be – and how young children learn and develop. A further key consideration stems from historical and cultural traditions and values. Different periods in history have been characterised by a unique set of circumstances which has affected the kinds of opportunities, materials and human resources available to young children in their daily lives, including their experiences in early childhood education settings. Within a single generation, there can also be huge variation depending on factors such as social class, religion, gender or geographical location. In our endeavour to illuminate the present issues and concerns influencing early childhood pedagogy, in this chapter we explore the various ways in which socio-historical contexts have influenced policy and practice in early education over time.

The first half of the chapter tracks the origins of early childhood pedagogy in Europe. It outlines some of the influential ideas of key individuals, such as John Locke, Jean Jacques Rousseau, Richard and Maria Edgeworth, Samuel Wilderspin, Friedrich Froebel, Maria Montessori, and Rachel and Margaret McMillan, and describes how they were interpreted in practice in early childhood education and care (ECEC) settings in Ireland. The second half of the chapter considers how ECEC policy and practice in Ireland has evolved from the 1970s to the present day.

Beginnings of early childhood pedagogy in Europe

In the history of child-rearing and education in Europe during the eighteenth century, two individuals stand out: firstly, John Locke (1632–1704), whose ideas are considered representative of the Age of Enlightenment, and, secondly, Jean Jacques Rousseau (1712–1778), whose writing is viewed as reflecting the new 'sensibilities' of the Romantic Age. Locke's collection of reflections on child-rearing, entitled *Some Thoughts Concerning Education* (1693), was based on the notion of the creation of the rational man through a controlled environment. It has been described as the principal child-guidance book of the eighteenth century, advising many middle-class families in the upbringing and education of their children (Cunningham, 1995; Hardyment, 1995). By presenting the image of child as a *tabula rasa*, or blank slate, Locke afforded the adult a position of great influence and responsibility in terms of moulding the child into the adult that the parent/tutor wished the child to become. Much emphasis was placed on moral education, virtue and bodily health. Significantly, Locke also recognised play as a natural disposition of childhood, proposing that the enthusiasm and energy that children demonstrated in their play could be channelled towards learning, thus paving the way for the notion of educational play and educational toys (Yolton & Yolton, 2000).

As industrialisation began to take hold in Western Europe at the end of the eighteenth century, the location and nature of daily activity for many working-class children moved from outdoors close to home to indoors, removed from the family environment in factories, mills and mines. It was in this context that Jean Jacques Rousseau wrote his famous treatise on education *Émile*, considered a founding text of Romanticism. The central emphasis of *Émile* was the assertion that the primary concern of all education should be the identity and particular nature of the child himself so that the child might achieve personal wholeness and be a 'good' human being. This would be achieved by controlling the environment of the child from birth, so his original nature could be preserved unspoilt, and by taking full account of the particular nature of the child at each stage in his development. Rousseau proclaimed both the child's innocence and the child's right to live a full life as a child. Unlike Locke, there was indifference to the vocation or profession the child would later follow. The preferred environment for Émile's education was the rural one, which would function as a retreat from the growing chaos and corruption revealed by the first wave of the Industrial Revolution and the massing of population in the new industrial cities in Europe. Rousseau's approach was an individualist approach to natural education. Ideally, Émile would be brought up without human contact at all, apart from the unobtrusive guidance of a tutor. In such an environment Nature was the principal guide, limiting what was physically possible at each stage of development and as motivator or guide to action and learning. A recurring theme in the first part of *Émile*, which addresses the period of infancy or birth to six years, is the centrality of sensing, movement and activity to learning. Less constrained children, according to Rousseau 'will remain more nearly in their natural state' (Rousseau, 1762, 177).

One individual in Ireland who was inspired by both Locke's and Rousseau's work was the Anglo-Irish landlord Richard Lovell Edgeworth, master of Edgeworthstown in County Longford. A liberal thinker, author, inventor and magistrate, Edgeworth was also an educationist. With his eldest daughter Maria, who was to become a renowned writer in her own right, Edgeworth wrote a more practical, common-sense text on the raising of children, entitled *Practical Education* (1798), aimed at the rising middle classes. The Edgeworths' work is an example of a more progressive approach to educational provision at the beginning of the nineteenth century that was initiated by members of the Anglo-Irish upper classes who could afford to travel in Europe as philanthropic tourists.

Writing of her father's educational aims, Maria Edgeworth wrote:

> *Surely, it would be doing good service to bring into a popular form all that metaphysicians have discovered which can be applied to practice in education. This was early and long my father's object. The art of teaching to invent – I dare not say, but of awakening and assisting the inventive power by daily exercise and excitement, and by the application of philosophic principles to trivial occurrences – he believed might be pursued with infinite advantage to the rising generation* (Hare, 1894, p.12).

Like Rousseau, the Edgeworths emphasised the importance of the early years in education and also referred to the importance of giving young children freedom to explore the environment through touch. They recommended careful selection of play props, 'Balls, pulleys, wheels, strings, and strong little carts, proportioned to their age, and to the things which they want to carry in them, should be their playthings' (Edgeworth & Edgeworth, 1798, vol. 1, p. 11). Encouraging children's curiosity about natural history early on was also urged and the tendency to constrain children's inquisitiveness and activity was criticised. Like Rousseau, the Edgeworths preferenced the rural over the urban as the setting for rearing children. Being brought out for a walk in the town in the company of servants was to be avoided at all costs, although they recognised children's delight in free time outdoors which often brought them to the city streets:

> *All the natural, and all the factitious ideas of the love of liberty, are connected with this distinct part of the day, the fresh air – the green fields – the busy streets – the gay shops – the variety of objects which the children see and hear – the freedom of their tongues – the joys of bodily exercise, and of mental relaxation, all conspire to make them prefer this period of the day which they spend with the footman, to any in the four and twenty hours* (Edgeworth & Edgeworth, 1798).

The visibly poor living conditions of the population in Ireland and the fear of general disorder prompted Richard L. Edgeworth to make a report to the Commissioners of Education in Ireland that was published in 1821. In his report, he proposed the intervention of the 'ladies of Ireland' who, he stated, were intent 'upon bettering the condition of the poor'. He writes: 'By their means Dame Schools may be provided as receptacles for young children, to habituate them to cleanliness, order and obedience, before they are sent to any of the preparatory day schools' (Edgeworth, 1821).

The *Dame Schools* Edgeworth referred to in his report had begun to be set up in Britain as an early form of day-care provision for the youngest children to free mothers to work as industrialisation's demand for labour increased. They have also been described as a form of 'mutual self-help arising within working-class culture' run by women in their own homes (Whitbread, 1972, p.7). Descriptions of Dame Schools tend to focus on the dirt, darkness and poor ventilation. As noted by Hartley (1993), the ad hoc arrangements of the Dame School did not fit the emerging middle-class view of what constituted a proper institution for children. However, an alternative form of provision began to emerge in the early decades of the nineteenth century in the growing numbers of industrial centres in Western Europe. This form of early childhood education provision was organised by the middle classes for the young children of poorer mothers forced into employment because of economic necessity. The French models, begun in Paris in the 1820s, were referred to as *salles d'asile* (translated as rooms of asylum), and were the forerunners of the *écoles maternelles*; the equivalent German models were the *kinderbewahranstalten*, also referred to as *kleinkinder schulen* (schools for young children); the Dutch had the *Bewaarscholen* (similar to the Dame Schools) and, beginning in the late 1860s, *Kleine kinder bewaarplaatsen* (day-care facilities for children of mothers forced to work out of economic necessity) (Tavecchio, 2005). The early British infant schools also fall into this category of provision which combined a charitable education through 'training in good habits'. They have been variously analysed in terms of humanitarian motives on the one hand, and social control on the other. The schools differed throughout Europe in some fundamental aspects. The French *salles d'asile* were staffed by women only, whilst the German *kleinkinder schulen*, in keeping with the strong male tradition in education in Germany, were staffed by men only. However, a common feature across all forms was the emphasis on order and cleanliness. Hartley (1993) links this focus to the wider trends of industrialisation, i.e. scientific rationality and bureaucracy.

Edgeworth's reference to the philanthropic role of 'the ladies of Ireland' is also significant in the history of early childhood pedagogy in Europe at this period. Philanthropy was one of the few activities that gave women access to the public arena without threatening its male domination. Through charity work, women of the upper and middle classes could alter their prescribed character, yet continue to act in the maternal 'virtuous' manner that was expected of them, in addition to enacting their roles as nurturers, care-givers and healers (Luddy, 1995; Preston, 1996; Clarke, 2000). In Ireland, denominational rivalry played a part in activities to relieve poverty, much of it focused on children (Luddy, 1998).

The first early childhood care and education settings in Ireland

One of the earliest ECEC settings to be established in Dublin was an infant school that was opened in 1824 in Westland Row. It was an initiative of a voluntary society comprising principally Protestant members who were supported and guided by an Englishman by the name of Samuel Wilderspin (1792–1866). At this time Wilderspin was making a name for himself as a promoter of infant education throughout the British Isles. Following the example set by factory owner and social reformer Robert Owen (1771–1858) in the provision of an infant school and playground in the model manufacturing village of New Lanark near Glasgow in 1816 (Owen, 1970), infant schools began to be set up by the middle classes and some members of the aristocracy in a bid to rescue children of the poor from the negative effects of city living (McCann & Young, 1982). A key figure in the promotion of the benefits of infant education at that time was MP Henry Brougham (later to become Lord Chancellor). In a parliamentary debate in 1820, he argued that the education of the poor was 'the best security for the morals, the subordination and the peace of the counties' (Parliamentary Debate, 28 June 1820, cited in McCann and Young, 1982). As the agent of the then established Infant School Society, Wilderspin travelled around Britain and Ireland during the 1820s at the request of any lady or gentleman to advise on the opening of infant schools. One such request came from Lady Powerscourt, who established an infant school for the children of the workers of the Powerscourt Estate in Enniskerry, County Wicklow. Wilderspin hoped that by teaching the children in the infant school cleanliness, kindness and self-control, the behaviour of the parents would be improved. During his 1833 and 1834 lecture tours in Ireland,

Wilderspin had publicly advocated the establishment of the Dublin Infant School Society and a model infant school. He was also quoted as saying that Ireland was peculiarly favourable to the spread of infant education because 'her children are the quickest I have ever met with' (Saunders News-Letter, 19 September 1833, cited in McCann & Young, 1982). Infant education, Wilderspin asserted, could contribute to the eradication of 'turbulence' from the Irish character and help the promotion of peace and order by giving 'the mental ascendancy over the physical'.

By the 1830s, the ruling British government was devising a much more comprehensive educational experiment for Ireland, in the form of a national school system. One of the proposals of the National Board of Education, which was established to operationalise the project, was the creation of an educational campus in Dublin with a training college, residential accommodation for trainee teachers and model schools (Coolahan, 1981). Wilderspin was invited to manage the project. Three model schools in separate blocks were erected in a line in a site on Marlborough Street between 1836 and 1838: a girls' school, a boys' school and, in the centre, an infants' school (O'Dwyer, 1992).

The pedagogical practices advocated by Wilderspin for the infant school were somewhat removed from the approach first advocated by Owen. Wilderspin believed that endless variety was critical for the developing mind of the child. Thus the school day was divided into short lessons on different subjects including instruction in letters and spelling, arithmetic, picture lessons on Scripture history, gallery lessons on natural history, geometrical figures and musical characters. These were interspersed with gymnastic exercises, marching and free play in the playground, which was given a prominent role in the school day. Wilderspin considered the presence of the teacher in the playground essential. He described his/her role as follows: to prevent accidents; to attend to moral and physical training; and to see that children acquired the habits of honesty and kindness to each other (Wilderspin, 1840). However, the choice of play should always be left to the children, for Wilderspin came to believe, just as Locke had, that if free to play as they chose, the child would 'show its character in its true light' (Wilderspin, 1840, p. 70).

Influential figures in the expansion of ECEC in the nineteenth and twentieth centuries

The demand for middle-class infant schools in Europe was largely unrealised until the beginning of the kindergarten movement which was led by Friedrich Froebel (1782–1852) and his followers. Froebel's distinctive pedagogy, in the form of the kindergarten, originated in the predominately rural German state of Thuringia in the 1830s. In founding the kindergarten in 1839, Froebel's attention was particularly focused on young children's activity and occupation drive, which could be expressed through shared play with trained adults – both parents and kindergarten teachers – typically women. There is a multitude of layered meanings to Froebel's 'garden' of children. It has been interpreted as a metaphor for the organic unity of the child and the universe, which positioned nature as mediator between God and man. It also reflects the protective, garden-like atmosphere that was considered the most appropriate context for the development of the inner and outer life of childhood. Kindergarten is also understood as a physical space, which incorporates an actual garden (Hoof, 1977; Liebschner, 1992; Steedman, 1990).

Early kindergartens in Ireland were private, few in number, and attended by middle-class children of the professional or business classes. The first, established in 1862 by the well-known German Froebelian, Eleonare Heerwart (1835–1911), was at the request of the Webbs, a prominent Quaker family in Dublin. Eleonare Heerwart trained as a kindergarten teacher under Froebel's wife, Luise Froebel, in 1853. In 1862 she moved to Dublin, where, until 1874, she operated a school on the Rathmines Road that incorporated a kindergarten. The school day was from 9 a.m. to 2 p.m., and the hour between 2 p.m. to 3 p.m. each day was set aside for meetings with teachers and preparations for the next day. Other kindergartens and schools subsequently set up in Ireland could be regarded as 'secondary acquisitions' (Wollons, 2000) in the sense that they largely imported the English kindergarten model, which had already gone through a process of transformation. A half-decade after the closure of Heerwart's school, another kindergarten opened nearby in Rathmines. This was the Rathgar Kindergarten and Junior School, which was founded by M. Isabel Douglas in 1919. Children from age four to twelve attended. According to a book published by the school, the curriculum for four-year-olds included 'training in observation of flowers and plants, insects and animals. They care for small gardens; they paint; they learn rhymes, poems and songs ...' (Montgomery, n.d).

Pioneers of girls' education and the subsequent development of girls' secondary education also became associated with the kindergarten movement in England and, in a few cases, in Ireland. Schools and colleges for women helped to expand the sphere of paid employment for middle-class women. Many schools had a kindergarten attached that functioned as a school for their youngest pupils as well as a place where their older pupils could be trained in kindergarten education (Brehony, 2003). There were two such examples in Dublin. Alexandra College was first established in 1866 as a training college for middle-class Protestant girls who wished to become governesses. In 1889, kindergarten classes for young children were started there. From 1918 until 1970, Alexandra College also provided kindergarten teacher training (O'Connor & Parkes, 1983). Likewise, the Dominican Convent on Eccles Street was set up in 1883 as an alternative to Alexandra College for girls of Catholic backgrounds. Some decades later, motivated by a need to staff their Catholic junior schools, the Dominican Order began training teachers in Froebel education, firstly in St Dominic's in Belfast in 1934, and then in Dominican College, Sion Hill, to where the training was transferred in 1943 and where it continues today (Liebschner, 1991).

In the second half of the nineteenth century, cities in Ireland continued to attract those seeking to escape famine and extreme poverty in rural areas. Living conditions in cities were very poor, however. Women were forced to work as dealers, washerwomen or domestic help. Children often worked, tending livestock, delivering milk or street-dealing (Johnston, 1985). A number of institutions and services that were established in a bid to rescue children in this period still exist today, although their form and function have changed. In 1887, *Miss Carr's Homes* was established to rescue destitute Protestant children who may have been orphaned, ill or dying. In 1893, the Society of Friends, the Quakers, opened a crèche on Meath Street in the Liberties, which was later named *The Liberty Crèche*, in order to care for the young children of married women forced to work to support their families. Catholic orders and congregations were also very active at this time and it was the female orders, by and large, both locally established and imported (principally from France), that had responsibility for young children and all girls (O'Sullivan, 2001; Prunty, 1999). Orphanages and industrial schools, many of which took in children under six years of age, were established. Parents committed their children to orphanages and industrial schools if they were widowed and unable to care for them. The Daughters of Charity, founded by St Vincent de Paul in France to care for the poorest of the poor, came to Dublin in 1855. Their first initiative was the establishment of a refuge for discharged Catholic women prisoners, where they hoped to turn them 'from their evil ways' (Prunty, 1999). In 1922 the Daughters of Charity opened St Mary's Day Nursery on Henrietta Street, which has been described as one of the first accredited nurseries in the new Irish State (Sr Monica Cowman, 2007).

Some years earlier, in 1907, Dr Maria Montessori (1870–1952) had established the first children's house (*casa dei bambini*) as part of San Lorenzo housing project in a slum area of the city of Rome. This initiative was to herald what Montessori herself referred to as the new 'scientific pedagogy'. The Montessori method was to become a very influential approach to early childhood pedagogy in many parts of Europe during the twentieth century. Montessori proposed an integration of an appreciation of the child's nature, which had been similarly captured in the educational philosophies of child-centred educationists and philosophers who preceded her, such as Comenius, Rousseau, Pestalozzi and Froebel, with a scientific approach to studying child behaviour. In Ireland, the Catholic Sisters of Mercy established the first Montessori classroom in the junior section of St Otteran's school, Philip Street, Waterford city in 1920. It was available free of charge to the poor and underprivileged children in the vicinity. This classroom was to become immortalised as the inspiration for W.B. Yeats's poem 'Among School Children'. Yeats visited St Otteran's in his capacity as a senator at a period when he was very interested in educational reform, particularly the developments in educational reform in Italy. Five years after the establishment of St Otteran's, another Montessori school opened in Waterford in the Ursuline Convent. Because of Montessori's Catholic background, the Dominican order was also attracted to her work, and opened a Montessori children's house in their junior school in Sion Hill, Blackrock, in 1928. By 1934, a Montessori training course had been established in Sion Hill, and Montessori herself came to examine the first group of students.

An unrelated development in Dublin that impacted on the daily lives of children living in the city in the 1930s was the establishment of a scheme for supervised play centres. This was the initiative of the *Civics Institute of Ireland,* which was a philanthropic organisation that comprised a group of people (men and women) who shared an interest in the development of civic spirit and improvement of amenities in Ireland's cities and towns and who worked in a voluntary capacity. An appeal for public money in support of the play centre initiative was made through a letter to *The Irish Times* on 6 October 1930. The appeal was made on the following three grounds:

- *Public health, because children must have suitable recreation under sanitary conditions.*
- *Public morals, because children who are happily playing under supervision will not ultimately become juvenile delinquents.*
- *Public safety, because children playing in the streets are a contributory cause of accidents and a danger to themselves and others* (Papers of Civics Institute of Ireland, Dublin City Archives, B12/7/1/0).

Between 1933 and 1939, ten playgrounds, staffed by trained play leaders, opened in various locations around the city (Kernan, 2005). They were open throughout the year when schools were closed, on weekday afternoons, weekends and during school holidays. An early plan was that the playgrounds could be opened in the morning as nursery playgrounds where working mothers could leave their preschool-aged children under trained supervision (Civics Institute of Ireland, Annual Report, 1935). However, with the realisation that the training required for supervisors working with the younger children in such a setting was lengthier, and therefore more costly than the ad hoc training that was being provided at that time for play leaders, two approaches seemed to have been adopted. Firstly, nursery sections with sand gardens within the main playgrounds were created. This was essentially a sunken pit in the ground filled with sand and equipped with buckets, spades and other loose play props. Playgrounds with infant sections also had small swings, wooden rockers and an external tap for water (Kernan, 2005).

A second scheme proposed was the development of nursery centres specifically for the care of preschool-aged children whilst their mothers worked. This scheme became the responsibility of the Ladies Committee of the Civics Institute in 1939. It was to the writings of social reformer and instigator of the nursery garden school, Margaret McMillan (1860–1931), and those who succeeded her in the *Nursery School Association of Great Britain*

and Ireland, that the committee principally drew on when planning commenced for a nursery centre. The new centre, called St Brigid's Nursery Centre, opened on 30 September 1940 in the old tennis pavilion on Mountjoy Square in Dublin.

It is clear that in the early days of its existence the members of the Civics Institute felt that the nursery centre was providing a substitute home: a stable and healthy home life which was perceived not to be possible in the living circumstances and conditions of the children's own homes, in most cases a one-roomed tenement accommodation. Middle-class ideals of a good or proper childhood are indicated in the following description of the nursery centre published by the Civics Institute of Ireland:

> *The centre is not a school – it is a large, airy nursery where these little boys and girls of the important and impressionable ages between 2½ and 4½ years lead a normal, happy family life. They play, eat and sleep at regular intervals just like children in more affluent circum-stances. They learn to eat their food in a mannerly way, to wash their hands before meals, tidy their hair, brush their teeth, and use the toilets as they should be used. In other words it is a Home for these 32 children* (Annual Report 1946–47).

In addition to a focus on children's physical welfare, the daily programme was designed to provide routine and training in social skills. Children arrived between 9 a.m. and 9.30 a.m. and went home at 5 p.m. The mornings began with prayers and breakfast, followed by practical life exercises and recreation between 10.15 a.m. and 11.30 a.m. This was followed by dinner and then sleep. While play outdoors was included in the daily routine, it appears to have had a lesser position in the overall programme compared to McMillan's nursery schools in England. According to records of the nursery from the 1940s, students taking the Diploma in Social

Science in Trinity College and University College Dublin, as well as students from the Froebel Training College in Alexandra College, Milltown and the Montessori College and Froebel College both run by the Dominican Sisters in Sion Hill Blackrock, undertook practical placements in the nursery centre. In 1955, the Civics Institute opened a second nursery centre in Morningstar Road, in the Coombe in Dublin city. The model of provision in these two nursery centres was to form the basis of other day nurseries established in the 1960s, 1970s and 1980s in various locations throughout the city that targeted children deemed to be 'at risk' or disadvantaged in some way. These were part-funded by the Dublin Health Authority, later to become the Eastern Health Board (now part of the Health Services Executive).

During the 1950s and 1960s, the ideals of the progressive child-centred approach associated with John Dewey (1859–1952) and Susan Isaacs (1885–1948), as well as the essential principles of Froebelian educational philosophy, began, to a certain extent, to influence views regarding pedagogical practices within the early years of the primary school in Ireland. This ideology included: exploration, discovery learning, hands-on experience, child-initiated activity, and the importance of choice, freedom and independence. Within such an ideology, child-directed play was afforded a central position. Some Irish educators began to be influenced by the so-called 'progressive movement' of child-centred education encapsulated in the influential Plowden Report in England, *Children and their Primary Schools* (1967). One of the channels of influence on State-supported primary education was through the work of the Dominican Order who began in a small way to demonstrate the applicability of a Froebelian child-centred approach to education in large classes in primary schools. For example, in the late 1940s the Archbishop of Dublin approached the Dominican Order, who at this stage were also offering training in Froebel education in Sion Hill, Blackrock, to ask if they would 'take on' the education of the children in Ballyfermot (Flanagan,

2004). At that stage Ballyfermot was one of Dublin's newest suburbs, built as part of Dublin Corporation's rehousing policy that
relocated hundreds of families from city-centre flats and tenements.
By the time the school was complete in the second half of the
1950s, it comprised seven separate schools in three large buildings,
the largest school in Europe at the time.

A key catalyst in this process was the vision and leadership of
educationalist Sr Simeon Tarpey, who was Head of the Froebel
Teacher Training College in Sion Hill, Blackrock in 1950s and
1960s. In a published lecture given in 1963, Sr Simeon identified
some of the main principles of 'modern teaching methods' which
were to pave the way for the very progressive *Curaclam Bunscoile*
(Primary School Curriculum) which was published by the
Department of Education in 1971. In this lecture (delivered to
an audience of nurse tutors), she spoke about the importance of
attention to the uniqueness of each individual child; a view of the
child as a member of society in which he must live and play a part;
the notion of holistic development; the significance of viewing
learning as a co-operative activity in which both pupil and teacher
have important parts to play ('activity on the part of the learner is
more important than activity on the part of the teacher, who in a
certain sense is subordinate to the pupil'); and, finally, the notion
of interest as sustained attention (Tarpey, 1963). When it was
published, the 1971 Primary School Curriculum was viewed as
radically different to what had existed previously. It recommended
that teachers use individual and group teaching rather than class
teaching methods with 'each child progressing at his own natural
rate, each at the different stages of his advancement being allowed
full scope to express his own personality and experience the joy of
discovery' (Department of Education, 1971, p.16).

Up to the late 1960s, most children in Ireland remained at home,
in the care of their mother, until they attended the junior infant
class of the local primary school at the age of four or five. However,
a number of socio-political developments across Europe began to

slowly impact on Ireland, including an expansion of and interest in ECEC provision and women's desire for an identity outside the home. Very gradually, other alternatives, for early socialisation began to become available, especially for three- to five-year-old children. Across Europe the form and function of ECEC provision varied from country to country, as it was heavily influenced by dominant political discourses regarding women's position in the workforce and whether or not ECEC was a public or private matter (Lamb, Sternberg, Hwang & Broberg, 1992).

In 1961, a young working mother in London, Belle Tutaev, wrote a letter to *The Guardian* newspaper, an event which is generally linked to the establishment of the preschool playgroup movement. In this letter Belle Tutaev described how, in the absence of a State nursery place for her daughter, she and a group of friends had set up a group of their own whereby they took turns as parents to provide play activities for each other's young children while the other mothers worked. Tutaev's offer to help others wishing to do the same eventually led to the establishment of the Preschool Playgroups Association (PPA) a year later. By the late 1960s, groups of similarly minded individuals interested in promoting ECEC experiences for all young children began to organise themselves in Ireland. One such forum was an Irish branch of Organisation Mondiale Education Prescolaire (OMEP), which was established in 1966 under the chairmanship of Dr Anne McKenna. Between 1967 and 1969 a series of seminars was held in Dublin, one of which was given by Belle Tutaev. These attracted a wide range of participants, including representatives of the various churches and religious orders, the Civics Institute of Ireland, health and education training colleges, health authorities, academics, and those working directly with young children (Sr Monica Cowman, 2007). One of the outcomes was the establishment of the Irish Preschool Playgroups Association (IPPA) in 1969 (Douglas, 1994). The single initiative instigated by the Department of Education at this time (1969), which focused specifically on the area of ECEC, was the preschool intervention project at Rutland

Street which was part-funded by the Bernard Van Leer Foundation, based in The Hague (Holland, 1979).

Organising and regulating ECEC provision: the interaction between the voluntary sector and the State 1970s–1990s

During the 1970s and 1980s there was a slow but steady development of early childhood services in Ireland to meet the growing demand of parents for part-time preschool provision, particularly for children of three years of age – just prior to the traditional school entry age of four. This service development was, until the 1990s, largely driven by the voluntary sector, in particular membership groups such as the Irish Preschool Playgroup Association and the Comhchoiste Réamhscolaíochta (Irish medium playgroups). The numbers of private crèches and nurseries also began to increase slowly and, in 1986, the National Children's Nurseries Association (NCNA) was established.

In addition, as described above, there had always been a philanthropic interest in developing family supports for disadvantaged children through charitable organisations such as the Civics Institute of Ireland, the Daughters of Charity and Barnardos. However, while these organisations did receive some State support for their work, the developments across the country were ad hoc and unregulated. The Child Care Act 1991 was a crucial piece of legislation, updating legislation from 1905 to bring Irish law into line with much of the practice in the social and health domain. The Act was significant in that it gave a legal definition of the child as under the age of eighteen and it focused on the protection and welfare of children and the responsibility of the State in this regard. Specifically, in relation to ECEC, this was the Act that created a national context within which ECEC settings were regulated and standards were established. Prior to the implementation of Section VII of the 1991 Act, early years services were unregulated and, despite parents and providers welcoming the regulations, there was some concern that they did not go far enough. The Act called for notification of intention to provide a service, but did not seek registration; there were limitations to the services covered so that many childminders were exempt (the exemption was determined by the number of children under the age of six years attending the service); and there was no requirement regarding the training and qualifications of those providing early years services. In 2006, amended regulations widened the services to be regulated but failed to move on either registration or qualifications.

Whilst the preschool regulations mark a very particular policy engagement with ECEC, there had been a growing attention to the issue from the mid-1980s with women's groups, unions and, latterly, employers calling on support for the development of childcare services to facilitate the participation of women in the workforce. Evidence of this growth of interest can be seen particularly in the partnership agreements (Hayes, 2002) and in a number of reports, specifically the Report of the Working Party on Child Care Facilities for Working Parents (1983) and the 1985 Report on Minimum Legal Requirements and Standards for Day-care Services (Department of Health, Unpublished).

In addition to the various reports, there were funding schemes available for developments in childcare. Although children, as a group, do not come within the legal competence of the EU, child-care was one of the sectors eligible for European funding under a number of different programmes, including equality initiatives such as the New Opportunities for Women (NOW) programme. Such funding led to the establishment of a number of pilot childcare projects at local and community level. These initiatives coincided with the work of the European Commission Childcare Network, which highlighted, among other things, the very low level of State support for childcare in Ireland when compared to all other European countries (European Commission Network on Childcare, 1990). Such information led to increased calls on the government for support and development of the sector, particularly among those who saw the potential value of childcare to disadvantaged children and their parents. By the early 1990s the impact of European reports, the recommendations from different working groups and the availability of funding began to yield a more concerted approach by interest groups in Ireland for policy action in relation to childcare. At this time, as a result of growing economic prosperity, there was an emerging drop in the unemployment rate that began to give rise to a shortage of workers. This led to employer organisations and unions adding their voice to demands for childcare, an identified barrier to the full participation of women in the labour force and a threat to sustainability of economic growth. Despite the variety of reports and recommendations, there was a very limited response at a political or practical level, as evidenced through, for example, the fact that childcare services in Ireland remained unregulated until January 1997.

Policy developments in the 1990s

It was not until the latter part of the 1990s that attention to childcare policy escalated to the top of the policy agenda. However, there were a series of initiatives from earlier in that decade that drove the increased impetus. One action – the establishment, through the Department of Education, of the Early Start Early Intervention Project in 1994 – did unsettle the status quo and caused the wider early education sector to review its position. The Early Start was established within the existing primary school system and supported the development of a network of preschool classes for three-year-olds in designated disadvantaged areas (Education Research Centre, 1998). The classes were staffed by primary teachers and childcare assistants and operated a curriculum reflective of the original Rutland Street intervention project of the late 1960s (Kellaghan, 1977; Kellaghan & Greaney, 1993). In addition, each classroom was provided with an equipment and material grant. The effect of this development on services outside the formal primary school system was reflected in the greater organisation of the not-for-profit preschool agencies and organisations that began to raise the profile of their services as potential sites for early intervention strategies. Among a number of initiatives at the time, an EU-funded project – the OMNA Dublin Institute for Technology/New Opportunities for Women (DIT/NOW) early childhood training project – offered an opportunity for the sector to come together and review childcare services, identify training requirements and develop, ultimately, a model framework for training and education for early years staff (OMNA, 2000; Department of Justice, Equality and Law Reform, 2002).

Interest in the policy potential of early childhood/childcare and the combined influences of the unions, businesses and the community at the *Partnership 2000* (1996) negotiations was highly significant for many sectors, but particularly so for children. The momentum that gathered on the issue of childcare ensured that it was included within the agreement as an area that needed to be addressed at policy level. While children do not feature in *Partnership 2000* as a constituency for specific policy consideration in themselves, they become visible in respect of wider policy issues such as social inclusion and equality. Attention is directed at the expansion and development of certain services for children. For instance, under the heading of combating educational disadvantage there are commitments to extending the Breaking the Cycle education initiative and to developing an early years intervention project for disadvantaged three- to four-year-olds. Under the heading of equality there is a commitment to support measures to develop the childcare sector so that parents, particularly women, have fewer barriers to accessing the labour market (Hayes, 2002).

In 1997, as a response to the *Partnership 2000* agreement, a widely representative working group, which included childcare providers as well as employers, unions and statutory representatives, met under the direction of the Department of Justice, Equality and Law Reform to produce a national strategy for childcare.

The focus of the report of the working group was the need for immediate attention to the supply-and-demand crises in childcare evident in Ireland at the time. The terms of reference of the group restricted attention to the childcare needs of working parents only. This was a serious limitation and guaranteed a fragmented policy response, as it did not allow for consideration of the wider issue of childcare for all children and their parents. This group considered the wide range of childcare services for children from birth to twelve years of age. This brought the sector of afterschool, as well as preschool and other forms of early childcare, into the policy arena for the first time and also included a review of the services offered by private childminders. The final agreed report of the working group was published in February 1999 and proposed a comprehensive seven-year strategy for the management and development of the childcare sector. This period coincided with the period of the National Development Plan 2000–2006.

On publication, the National Childcare Strategy (1999) was broadly welcomed. However, the government was somewhat cautious about accepting the recommendations in isolation from other policy documents. As a result, the publication of the strategy led to the formation of an interdepartmental group, under the direction of the Department of Justice, Equality and Law Reform, to review the recommendations alongside those of the Report of the Commission on the Family (1998), the Report of the National Forum on Early Childhood Education (1998) and the White Paper, *Ready to Learn* (1999). In July 1999, a National Childcare Coordinating Committee was established, again under the Department of Justice, Equality and Law Reform, to commence the implementation of aspects of the National Childcare Strategy. The National Development Plan allocated over €400m through the Equal Opportunities Childcare Programme (EOCP) to facilitate the development of the childcare sector. The EOCP funding covered areas of capital investments, staffing grants for settings in disadvantaged communities, innovation supports and the establishment of the National Coordinating Childcare Committee. Funding was also released to support the establishment of local city and county childcare committees, linked to the National Coordinating Childcare Committee and strengthened through the national voluntary organisations. An interim report of the EOCP (2003) concluded that the performance of the EOCP was disappointing and constrained by the requirement to meet the dual objectives of increasing the supply of childcare places for children of working parents and promoting social inclusion through provision of affordable childcare.

Alongside the EOCP investment, the Department of Health and Children established a preschool inspectorate to implement the 1996 preschool regulations. Inspection teams were established across the country over the period 1997 to 2000 and comprised public health nurses and environmental health officers. However, concern was expressed about the nature of the regulations and the inspectorate in that the focus was, initially, on health and safety, with little attention to the developmental needs of children, the daily routine or curriculum and the qualifications or training of the staff. Within the revised regulations of 2006, these limitations continue with no requirement on staff to have a qualification in the field.

The new century has seen some important developments, which have confirmed ECEC as a serious policy issue in Ireland. The growth of local childcare support networks and the broadening of influence of the collective national voluntary organisations have given a visibility and credibility to the sector that was missing in the 1990s. In addition, two important external reports on early childhood care and education have had an impact – one from the OECD (2004) and the other from the National Economic and Social Forum (2005). A structural development of potential was the establishment – in 2006 – of the Office of the Minister for Children (OMC) where there has been an effort to bring about cohesion and integration across a variety of policy issues that impact directly on children's lives through, in relation to ECEC, relocating the childcare section from the Department of Justice, Equality and Law Reform to the Department of Health and Children and the co-location of a number of units within the one office. These include the Youth Justice Section from the Department of Justice, Equality and Law Reform and the newly established Early Years Education Policy Unit from the Department of Education.

At a national level the publication of *Síolta – The National Quality Framework* (CECDE, 2006), and *The Framework for Early Learning* (NCCA, forthcoming) create a rich basis for considering the real integration of care and education in services for young children. Finally, the attention to the quality of staff working in the sector and the training initiative promised in the 2006 budget offers an opportunity to support and develop a graduate-led diverse professional base to enhance the quality of service provision and the experiences of young children.

Despite the various policy documents and the increased levels of investment, there continue to be dilemmas, difficulties and restrictions to the development of a comprehensive quality ECEC system for young children in Ireland. Some of these are outlined below and are intended to form the basis for discussion rather than simply as a critique of the current situation.

The focus on women at work: The terms of reference of the EOCP made it clear that investment in the development of childcare services was primarily intended to overcome a barrier to the full participation of women in the labour market. Taking this focus, rather than a child-centred focus, has influenced the way in which services are developed and supported. It has also compounded the as yet unresolved conflict between the traditional ideology of the family and the economic necessity to attract women into the workforce (Hayes, 2002; Hayes & Bradley, 2006).

A targeted versus a universal approach: As with so many of our social policies in Ireland, the approach to the development and support of the ECEC sector has been to focus most investment on services for disadvantaged families and children. While no one could dispute the fact that services provided in areas of disadvantage need additional supports, there is some question as to the value of targeting early childhood services in the absence of a universal policy on the sector. To some extent the sectoral collaboration that has been a feature of developments such as the publication of the *Model Framework* (DJELR, 2002), *The National Quality Framework* (CECDE, 2006) and *The Framework for Early Learning* (NCCA, forthcoming), has created a momentum across diverse settings that is universal and, as such, may provide the path towards a more complete attention to all services experienced by young children.

Centre-based institutional childcare over mixed-service developments: With such extensive funding available for investment in creating more childcare 'spaces', there has been a robust response from the building industry and a rapid development of centre-based full-day childcare without the concomitant development of smaller, sessional services and family-based childcare. This trend has continued despite the available information which suggests that Irish families would prefer a wider choice of settings for young children with different preferences across different ages and family requirements. The danger of the 'corporatisation' of early childhood services (Sumsion, 2006) that accompanies a market-led approach to service development should not be underestimated and is a cause for concern.

Parental funding versus sectoral support: The decision to commit €350m exchequer funding annually from 2006 to assist all parents of children under six years of age in buying childcare through the Early Years Supplement is one that will do nothing to strengthen the early childhood sector or improve and sustain quality. This crude measure was guided more by an attempt to treat all parents equally than by any commitment to improve and maintain the quality of the early education experiences of young children, and there is no guarantee that the supplement will be used to fund the early education of young children at all. Had that money been directed towards the services themselves – through, for instance, a quality linked-fee subsidy scheme or a capitation system – it would have marked the beginning of addressing the sustainability of a quality ECEC system. It seems that the need to treat all families the same in terms of investment in childcare, rather than addressing the rights and needs of young children attending early childhood services, dominated, and this may well be a decision that will be regretted in the future.

Childcare versus Early Education: Historically, we have, in Ireland, structurally separated childcare from early education in our policy development. The importance of approaching service development in an integrated way has been noted many times (DES, 1999; Hayes, 1995, 2001, 2002; NCCA, 2004; NESF, 2005; OECD, 2004) and yet, within the recently established Office of the Minister for Children, there is a separate Childcare Section and a separate Early Years Education Policy Unit. Were there a serious attempt being made to integrate care and education, the National Childcare Investment Programme would have been titled the National Programme for Investing in Children's Services and the units developing and implementing early childhood policies would have been merged. (The above section was taken from N. Hayes, 2007.)

From reflection to refocusing

This last decade has shown a growth in investment in early childhood education and care and an increase in the number of places and settings, although the demand still outstrips supply. There has been a growth and refinement of structures with the creation of the OMC and the establishment of an Early Years Education Policy

Unit within the Department of Education and Science. However, the resolution of problems of access and affordability has been limited, with a large population of children who would benefit from early educational experiences unable to access them. Furthermore there has been a minimal development of sustainable, high-quality settings for young children and their families with the integration of childcare and early education still in its earliest stage. This latter concern is exacerbated by the limited growth of a well-trained professional body to provide and maintain quality services. This opportunity for reflection confirms the view that we have yet to place the young child at the centre of our policy development and, until such time as we do that, we may be compromising the rights of children to quality ECEC, and correspondingly compromising their development, through the desire for expediency, ambivalence and the economically driven pressure to increase childcare places for working parents.

SUMMARY

In this chapter a number of disparate elements in the history of ECEC in Ireland from the early nineteenth century up to the present day have been weaved together to provide a coherent account of its development. The influence of key individuals from the world of philanthropy and from religious organisations on the kinds of ECEC provision made available to young children in Ireland has been highlighted, as has the impact of more radical thinkers and social reformers. Themes addressed in the review of the more distant past include the attention to young children's 'natural' dispositions in ECEC provision, including activity drive, movement, sensing and play; the view of ECEC as central to social reform, particularly with regard to ameliorating poverty; reforming the child-rearing habits of the 'children of the poor', and bringing order and control to perceived disorder in society; and the role of ECEC in extending the sphere of women's work. The analysis of the more recent past has identified a number of key concerns that highlight the fact that children's interests have yet to be placed centre stage in ECEC policy. It is acknowledged that within the limitations of a single chapter it is necessary to be selective. Whilst many contributions have been described, it has been impossible to give voice to all the individual and collective efforts and events that have contributed to change and transformation of ECEC over time.

Point for reflection

Consider the role of philanthropic, religious and voluntary organisations and the State in ECEC in Ireland over time and identify the features of ECEC in Ireland that mark its particularity compared to other contexts in Europe. Is it possible for you to identify a historical basis for why you do things in a certain way in ECEC settings? How is this way of working meaningful for the children and families you currently work with? Consider other ways of working.

Chapter three

Multiple Perspectives on Early Childhood Education and Care

INTRODUCTION

Understanding how cultures image their children can provide a basis for understanding cultural practices and policies that deal with children, including early childhood education and care (ECEC). On the one hand, child-rearing practices and pedagogical work with children reflect social values, expectations and aspirations for children; on the other hand, images also spark these practices, wishes and desires for children (Sigel, 1996). Images of childhood have been variously construed as conceptions, constructions, perceptions and shared beliefs about children. For more than a century the language of child development and developmental psychology has dominated commonly held constructions of childhood within the context of early childhood education. These include: the existence of innate tendencies or dispositions; the susceptibility to external influences; the limits of human modifiability; the special importance of early experience; and the role of the individual (Lamb & Hwang, 1996). However, learning and thinking are increasingly being conceptualised as social activities and children are viewed as competent, social, active agents in their learning and development alongside adults. In recent decades theoretical work in ECEC has also paid attention to the contexts of learning and development and the role played by communities and societies, including local and national governments, in shaping the context in which learning takes place.

This chapter reviews current theoretical constructs and images of childhood underpinning early childhood pedagogy. It broadens the discussion beyond child development theory by drawing on multidisciplinary perspectives in early childhood studies. Dominant images of the young child pervasive in the last quarter of the twentieth century are discussed in relation to how they influenced ECEC pedagogy. The chapter also introduces emerging concepts in ECEC discourse – such as place, space and time, children's rights, democracy and citizenship – and describes how these have influenced new understandings of ECEC, both nationally and internationally.

Transforming the twentieth-century child from child as 'object of study and investment' to 'child citizen' with rights and responsibilities

In the course of the twentieth century, children came to the fore as a point of intervention in and investment for the future needs of the State in many Western countries. New policies, institutions and various other 'provisions' for children – including nurseries, kindergartens, public health clinics, baby clubs, playgrounds and schools – increasingly drew on 'scientific' knowledge to inform practice. The emerging discipline of child development provided an important knowledge base for those concerned with the care and education of young children (Burman, 1994; James, 2001). The notion of children's natural 'nature', which had underpinned the educational philosophies of eighteenth- and nineteenth-century progressive educators such as Rousseau, Pestalozzi and Froebel, was given scientific legitimacy through the identification of what were considered universal stages of children's natural development. Within such a frame of reference, 'childhood' was understood as a biologically defined category, marked most simplistically by chronological age, underlining the fact that children are younger and less mature adults. Children everywhere, or 'the universal child', were seen as progressing from dependence to adulthood through stages or phases in an ordered, predictable and rule-governed way.

The pervasive image of the young child that accompanied such an understanding was that of a passive, needy, immature, dependent and naturally incompetent and incapable individual (Qvortrup, 1995). Children, as 'other' or 'less-than-adults', were also viewed as having the right to a childhood of innocence and freedom from the responsibilities of the adult world. One of the means of ensuring such a childhood was to provide a protected and separate space for childhood activity, learning and play as in a kindergarten, day nursery or preschool playgroup.

The study of child development, located within the broader framework of developmental psychology, became a central focus in most professional training courses in early childhood education. Early childhood practitioners were trained to look for developmental progression or 'signs of maturing' within motor, language and play behaviours. Children whose development or play behaviours didn't match 'normal' developmental milestones and competencies at particular ages were labelled as immature, deficient or developmentally delayed. By the 1960s, a policy of compensatory early education that targeted children who were considered particularly needy or 'at risk' in terms of their early learning and development due to disadvantaged home backgrounds, was initiated in many Western countries. One such example in Ireland was the Rutland Street Preschool Project referred to in Chapter 2. Throughout the 1970s and 1980s, pedagogical theories in early childhood were characterised by the view that curricula should be informed by understanding about developmental levels and the interests of each child (McNaughton, 2003). By the end of the 1980s, the notion of 'developmentally appropriate practice' (DAP), as set out in a document published by the National Association for the Education of Young Children (NAEYC) (Bredekamp, 1987) in the United States, was becoming influential and became a powerful construct and reference point in early childhood pedagogical practice. It appeared to offer early years practitioners a way of working that was based on 'scientific certainty', or indisputable evidence of what works. At a time when the search for quality was becoming a key influence on ECEC, the notion of 'developmentally appropriate practice' also came to represent universally agreed standards for quality in ECEC.

However, around the time of the initial publication of *Developmentally Appropriate Practice in Early Childhood Programmes serving Children from Birth through Age 8* (Bredekamp, 1987) the dominance of developmental theory in studies of childhood in general, and ECEC in particular, began to be challenged, both from within the field of developmental psychology itself and from the wider emerging field of social studies of childhood (Burman, 1994; Cannella, 1997; Dahlberg, Moss & Pence, 1999; James, Jenks & Prout, 1998; Woodhead, 1996). One of the criticisms raised was that developmental psychology was overly focused on age-related competency and deficits and that it failed to adequately describe and understand children's ordinary everyday lives, with all their complexities and ambiguities, as well as children's active participation in their social worlds (Hogan, 2005). Contemporaneously, there was a growing acknowledgment that 'child development' reflected a minority of world childhoods based principally on North-American and European childhoods as studied from the perspectives of North-American and European researchers (Woodhead, Faulkner & Littleton, 1998).

Towards the end of the 1990s the thinking and writing of key individuals within the strengthening field of ECEC academic research began to be characterised by a growing critical and reflective stance, and a number of 'taken for granted truths' that had underpinned the work of early years practitioners began to be questioned. Questions – such as where have these 'truths' come from? Who has generated them? Whose interests do they serve? What do we actually want for our children? – were being posed by writers in the field such as Woodhead (1996); Cannella (1997); Penn (1997); Dahlberg Moss & Pence (1999); and McNaughton (2000; 2003). Critiques of the conventional theorising in ECEC were also imbued by growing cross-disciplinary perspectives and the blurring around the edges of disciplines such as anthropology, education, geography, history, philosophy and sociology as well as developmental psychology. This was beginning to offer new ways of viewing and researching childhood and children's experiences in ECEC settings.

Sociological studies of childhood began to focus attention on childhood and children's lives and culture as worthy of study in their own right and not just in relation to the family. Replacing the traditional notion of socialisation, which focused on children's internalisation of adult skills and knowledge (a primarily passive role), childhood began to be viewed as a social 'construction' resulting from the collective actions of children with adults and with each other (Corsaro, 2005). There was also recognition of the fact that children are the primary source of knowledge about their experiences (Alderson, 2000; Corsaro, 2005; Devine, 2003; Mayall, 2002). A philosophy of listening began to underpin practice and research with children, including children in their earliest years (Alderson, 1995; Clark, Kjørholt & Moss, 2005). Qualitative research methodologies such as ethnography, trad-itionally used by anthropologists in their study of distant and 'exotic' peoples and cultures, began to be utilised by sociologists and educational researchers, providing children with a more direct voice and participation in the production of data as well as capturing the flow and the complexities of children's daily lives in settings such as

ECEC institutions (Clark, Kjørholt & Moss, 2005; Greene & Hill, 2005; Warming, 2005).

Much of Barbara Rogoff's work was derived from anthropological and ethnographic fieldwork amongst communities in Mexico, Guatemala, East Africa and India as well as the United States. Building on Vygotsky's socio-cultural view of development, she conceptualised development as a process of transformation of participation in socio-cultural activities. Rogoff's (2003) work and the work of other researchers – such as Goncu and Gaskins (2006); Gillen and Cameron (2003); Penn (2001); and Tobin, Wu & Davidson (1989) – have drawn attention to the diversity of values and goals in child-rearing and pedagogical practices cross-culturally, including: the degree of separation of children from community life; the segregation of children into same-age groupings; and the relationships between parents and children in play. By the close of the twentieth century, there was also a greater appreciation of the fact that the goals of child-rearing practices in many Western developed societies related primarily to personal, intellectual, social and political autonomy, becoming independent and self-sufficient, and that this was at odds with values such as interdependence, collaboration and integration, which are valued in the upbringing of children and prioritised in other societies (Woodhead, Faulkner and Littleton, 1998; Tobin, Wu & Davidson, 1989).

Within the sociology of childhood, the competing concepts of structure and agency have been usefully applied in understanding the experiences of children in institutions such as ECEC settings and primary schools (Devine, 2003; James *et al.* 1998; Kjørholt & Tingstad, 2007; Mayall, 2002). Structure refers to the manner in which society regulates and influences human behaviour at a macro level through its social organisation and involves the development of a shared commitment to certain ideologies, policies or established practices (Devine, 2003; Mayall, 2002). Pedagogical work in ECEC settings is the principal means through which society regulates and influences young children's behaviour and, as suggested in the introduction to this chapter, can be understood as reflecting social values and adults' expectations and aspirations for children. One form of structure is the almost universal feature in primary schools and in many ECEC settings of grouping children in tightly limited age cohorts, where expectations for development and behaviour are based on age (Rogoff, Correa-Chávez, Navichoc & Cotuc, 2005).

A competing concept to the notion of structure is that of children's agency, which emphasises children's competence as social actors and as active beings in the creation of their own life worlds (Devine, 2003). An individual child's agency to effect change may alter that child's experience of childhood, but it may also change childhood itself more generally by transforming adults' behaviours and perceptions (James & James, 2004). It is also noteworthy that the recent OECD (2006) report, *Starting Strong II*, highlights the importance of respecting children's agency and natural learning strategies. However, children's agency has to be understood within the parameters of childhood's minority status, where childhood is understood as a period of protection, implying provision and unequal power relationships between adulthood and childhood (Mayall, 2002). Drawing on gender studies, Alderson (2005) draws a comparison between the minority and weak status of children to that of women. She writes, 'Children often seem weak and ignorant because they are kept in helpless dependence. They are not allowed to gain knowledge and experience, or to show their strengths' (Alderson, 2005, p.131). The tension between structure and agency in children's lives, i.e. the extent to which children's behaviour and identity are shaped by social norms and rules, or the extent to which they are able to construct their own path and spaces where they can be firmly in control, has become a central interest to social theorists. One aspect of this has been in the consideration of the temporal and spatial frameworks of childhood. Here the academic field of geography and the 'new' geography of children has added richness and depth to our understanding by exploring geographical dimensions of children's lives, including the intersection of human and physical worlds and of time and space, spatial variation, the importance of scale, the distinctiveness of place and the meanings attached to significant sites of everyday life (McKendrick, 2000). Let us explore how such a perspective may be applied in ECEC contexts.

Considering space, place and time in early childhood education and care settings

The field of *geography of childhood* has emerged from a blurring of the edges around disciplines such as anthropology, environmental psychology and architecture, as well as sociology of childhood, and has much to offer ECEC. Spatiality incorporates region, movement, distance, proximity and, as noted by James *et al.* (1998) and Qvortrup (1995), the social space of childhood is interlinked with temporality. For example, age and changes in the material or biological body increase access to space (Hillman, Adams & Whitelegg, 1990; Newson & Newson, 1976). Norms and practices governing space and time in one arena can impact on others (Christensen & O'Brien, 2003). This is illustrated in the fact that the rhythms of young children's daily lives, in particular their access to time and space, are often dictated by the rhythms of adults' lives – the workplace and transport systems (Ennew, 1994). At the same time, the temporal frameworks of children's lives are, in part, patterned by the temporal flow or rhythms of children's own play and activity (James *et al.* 1998). A number of researchers, as well as key policy documents and curricula, have emphasised the importance of early years practitioners tuning into and respecting the rhythms of children's play and activity in early childhood settings (Bruce, 1996; David, Goouch, Powell & Abbott, 2002; Kernan, 2007; Moss & Petrie, 2002; National Children's Office, 2004). David *et al.* (2002) suggest that schedules and routines must 'flow with the child'.

Initially, geographies of children were primarily conducted on an individual level and have focused on the physical and social significance of individuals' experience of spaces, places, environments and landscapes. These revealed the differential possibilities for engagements with space, place, environment and landscape that are open to children living different childhoods (Hart, 1979; Moore, 1986). The first decade of the twenty-first century has also seen the emergence of macro-level studies which have focused on how the 'external' structuring of childhood, referred to previously, impacts on children's use of space (examples include: Christensen & O'Brien, 2003; Coninck-Smith & Gutman, 2004; Fog Olwig & Gulløv, 2003; Karsten, 2002; Zeiher, 2003). For instance, the reduced independent mobility for children outdoors in urban areas (Hillman *et al.* 1990) has been linked to the phenomena of 'insularisation'. This concept is used to describe how children spend much of their time within the confines of 'islands', such as houses, day-care settings or recreation centres, between which they are escorted and ferried by adults (Zeiher, 2003; Karsten, 2002). The combination of the insularisation and domestication of children (Mayall, 2002) means that many children are confined and controlled within houses and other sheltered places (Zeiher, 2003) and depend on their parents to transport them to explore activity options (Lareau, 2003). Anthropologists note that the social place of children in rural societies in developing countries is not as compartmentalised spatially as it is in typically urbanised and industrialised societies (Nieuwenhuys, 2003). This is illustrated in Nieuwenhuys' description of children's places in Poomkara, a village in Southern India.

> *I walked over workplaces, bathing and toilet areas, backyards and children's playgrounds, often unaware of boundaries other than an occasional palm-leaf stuck in the ground, a few low shrubs planted in a row, a simple piece of coir yarn tied between two coconut palms or even*

nothing more than signs drawn on the sandy ground.
Children's tiny kitchens of leaves and sand, the little holes
into which marbles had to be tossed, or the imaginary
roads on which palm-leaf cars were made to ride were
largely invisible unless one was bent upon questioning
every inch of children's local landscape. (Nieuwenhuys,
2003, p.103).

Kernan's interdisciplinary study examined how space, place and time
dimensions interacted with young children's lives to create opportunities to play outdoors in a range of ECEC settings in the city and
suburbs of Dublin (Kernan, 2006). The rationale for taking such an
approach was that it was not sufficient to examine the ECEC setting
alone in order to understand young children's experience of the outdoors. Rather, a richer and more 'authentic' analysis of the outdoors
was provided by exploring the whole day, from waking to sleeping;
whole weeks, including weekends; a whole year incorporating seasonal change and changes in personal circumstances. Viewing outdoor experiences this way allowed the realities of young children's
everyday lives, negotiated between home, ECEC settings and the
spaces 'in between' and all the complexities and ambiguities that
entails, to be captured (Hogan, 2005; Warming & Kampmann,
2007). The 'day-in-the-life' accounts of the participating children in
this study illustrated how individual personal characteristics, material circumstances and personal resources (adults' and children's) in
the immediate environments of the home and ECEC setting, as well
as broader structural factors, all interact and have a bearing on the
content of young children's experiences of the outdoors in their daily
lives. Each arena, home and ECEC setting had its distinct daily
ritualised routines. As noted by one of the fathers interviewed, these
were 'two different worlds, different rules seem to apply'. This
double socialisation for children (Greene & Hill, 2005) illustrates
the complexity of their lives, whereby children had to adapt quickly
to various rhythms governing their daily experiences.

Different opportunity structures existed that were unique to each child, marking variation in their experience of the outdoors. These were not static but changed over time by virtue of the children's changing development and learning, their personal and family circumstances and seasonal time. Ultimately, the overriding concern for all parents interviewed was 'to do the right thing' for their children. This often necessitated negotiations and trade-offs between children and adults, between home and ECEC settings, between what was good for the individual or for the group. The rhythm of the day for children, including time and space to play outdoors, was often determined by a complex conflation of parental work times, institutional routines, children's rhythms of rest and activity, and the time of year. Children's ability to shape their play environment varied according to their development, in particular their independent mobility and their ability to communicate their preferences, and the degree to which adults were 'in tune' with and responsive to children's interests. A further factor related to what was deemed 'acceptable', whether at home or in ECEC settings. For example, the question of young children climbing to heights higher than ground level, whether on slopes, low walls or pieces of furniture, was dealt with differently by different adults (Kernan, 2006). As noted by Reed (1996), the relationship between place and doing is not absolute. For example, one could run and make noise indoors, but one *ought* not to do so.

From structure and agency to interdependence

A further interesting development in childhood studies debates in the first decade of the twenty-first century is the problematising of the notion of children's agency and competency, including consideration of children in their early childhood years, with a suggestion that there is a danger in romanticising children's agency in their everyday lives (Dahlberg, 2005; Halldén, 2005; Warming & Kampmann, 2007). In response, the notion of 'interdependence' appears to be entering the ECEC discourse. Dunne (2005), for example, proposes the concept of interdependency with others as a solution to the distance between the adult of logical thought and the sensing, playing, exploring child. Halldén (2005) emphasises children's need for trustworthy, helpful and mature adults – a point addressed by Dahlberg (2005) in her description of an 'ethics of encounter', characterised by responsibility for others, trust and interdependability. Additionally, the new focus on the child as 'being-in-the-world' of everyday life is accompanied by an acknowledgement that children encounter the world, including their experiences of ECEC, in an idiosyncratic manner which can be different if they are boys or girls, as a result of their ethnicity, or due to the types of physical environments available to them in their everyday lives (Greene & Hill, 2005). This has been supported by findings from large-scale cross-national reviews and comparisons of early childhood education such as the IEA Preprimary Project (Weikart, 1999; Weikart, Olmsted & Montie, 2003), the OECD *Starting Strong I* and *II* (OECD, 2006), as well as the UNICEF *State of the World's Children* reports, which have drawn attention both to the variation and inequalities in children's early educational experiences globally. This has been accompanied by a call for respect for diversity in cultural 'norms' and values and a recognition that there are multiple perspectives and paradigms for viewing children's learning and development that should be taken into account when considering 'appropriate' or 'quality' early childhood education. Arising from these developments is the emergence of a discourse of equity, rights, social justice and respect for diversity in ECEC discourse.

Thus, at the beginning of the twenty-first century, studies of childhood are paying greater attention to the plurality of childhoods, evidenced cross-culturally, but also within cultures. The acknowledgement of the diversity of childhoods – constructed by different societies and generations, in different places and historical periods – is growing, allowing the possibility to rethink our conceptions of the education and nurturing of young children. An important development, in both sociology of childhood and developmental psychology, is a shift from viewing children as 'becoming' to 'beings' (Greene & Hill, 2005). Within developmental psychology, the importance of interactional and reciprocal relations in human-environment interactions (Moore, 1985) and the broader cultural context for learning and development (Bronfenbrenner, 1979; Bruner, 1996; Hogan, 2005; Vygotsky, 1978) is commanding greater attention. Thus, to an increasing extent, researchers and practitioners draw on socio-ecological or cultural-ecological models when considering children's experiences in ECEC settings. The consequence of this is that the previous dominant image of the child as passive, needy and innocent is being replaced progressively by an understanding of the young child as active, competent, eager to engage with the social and physical world, as an active agent in the developmental process, and in the creation of their own life worlds in interdependent relations with trusted adults. Reflecting this shift in thinking, the image of the young child presented in the National Council for Curriculum and Assessment's (NCCA) consultative document *Towards a Framework for Early Learning* and *The Framework for Early Learning* (NCCA, forthcoming) is that of a capable and active learner. Supporting this image is the identification of play and relationships as the two primary contexts for learning, thus emphasising the highly interactive and social nature of learning.

Towards a rights–based framework for early childhood pedagogy

Contemporaneous with the 'deconstruction' and 're-conceptualising' of ECEC during the 1990s and 2000s was a rapid expansion of services worldwide. Investing in the early years education increasingly became a policy concern of governments, and ECEC came to be viewed as a panacea for problems ranging from poverty, inequality, juvenile delinquency, marriage breakdown and unemployment. The notion of 'social capital' (Bourdieu, 1993) progressively began to gain currency. This focused attention on the cultural, social and emotional resources and information residing in the immediate social supports surrounding young children, i.e. parents, ECEC settings and other networks in the community (Farrell, Tayler & Tennent, 2003; 2004). The benefits of integrated services for young children and families were, and continue to be, linked to a social capital framework. Two further key developments that began to influence the policy discourse were: firstly, new findings within the field of brain research, and, secondly, the almost universal ratification of the United Nations Convention on the Rights of the Child (UNCRC, 1989). Let us examine each of these developments in turn.

Policy documents rely predominantly on positivistic or scientific evidence in setting out the rationale for investing in early childhood education (Moss, 2007). The scientific argument for early intervention is now bolstered and perceived as having greater legitimacy by new findings coming from neuroscience and understandings about brain development and functioning during the early years (Shonkoff & Phillips, 2002). However, there are contested views regarding how this knowledge can or should be applied in ECEC (Bruer, 1999; Zero to Three, 1999). The various dimensions of a causal relationship between positive early experiences and favourable developmental outcomes is illustrated in 'From Neurons to Neighbourhoods', compiled by a high level group of 'experts' and published in 2000:

(i)   *the importance of early life experiences, as well as the insep-arable and highly interactive influences of genetics and environment, on the development of the brain and the unfold-ing of human behaviour;*

(ii) *the central role of early relationships as a source of either support and adaptation or risk and dysfunction;*

(iii) *the powerful capabilities, complex emotions, and essential social skills that develop during the earliest years of life; and*

(iv) *the capacity to increase the odds of favourable developmental outcomes through planned interventions* (Shonkoff & Phillips, 2000, 1–2).

The principal arguments used by politicians, public policy analysts and educationalists, which have specifically drawn upon findings made possible by technological advances in brain imaging techniques, have been summarised by Smidt (2006). Here she also draws attention to the erroneous/faulty assumptions that have followed:

- *that the brain is at its most plastic and malleable in the early years of life – leading to the assumption that development during those years will last throughout life;*
- *that the connections made between neurons come about through stimulation – leading to the conclusion that, since stimulation in the early years will last forever and it is mothers and primary care-givers who provide this stimulation, they can be trained to ensure the child is exposed to an 'enriched' environment; and*
- *that the synaptic connections made in the first years of life are critical in determining later cognitive abilities (Smidt, 2006, p.124).*

Amongst the cautionary notes linked to the use of brain research in ECEC policy is that the importance of cognitive stimulation is scientifically unproven and very culturally bound (Bruer, 1999). Oftentimes the notion of an 'enriched' environment has come to be understood as offering children something Western, middle-class, implying expensive child-specific materials and objects (Smidt, 2006).

During the past decade and a half, the notion of children's rights, articulated with reference to the United Nations Convention on the Rights of the Child (UNCRC, 1989), has been instrumental in providing a tool for change, and has been used by children's advocates in their efforts to draw policymakers' attention to the need for accessible and inclusive ECEC services. The ratification of UNCRC by 192 governments (two countries have yet to ratify the convention: Somalia and the US) can be viewed as setting the scene for a new twenty-first century focus on pedagogical work with children in the form of a rights-based and social justice framework, underpinned by the respectful implementation of the articles of the UNCRC.

The Convention provides a comprehensive framework comprising 54 articles in total. The articles can be viewed in three categories – those dealing with *Provision, Protection* and *Participation* – although these should be seen as interdependent. The *Provision* articles recognise the social rights of children to minimum standards of health, education, social security, physical care, family life, play, recreation, culture and leisure. The *Protection* articles uphold the right of children to be safe from discrimination, physical and sexual abuse, exploitation, substance abuse, injustice and conflict. Finally, the *Participation* articles deal with civil and political rights, such as the right to a name and identity, the right to be consulted and taken account of, the right to physical integrity, the right to access to information, the right to freedom of speech and opinion and the right to challenge decisions made on their behalf (Lansdown, 1994).

The UNCRC has been of major significance in enhancing children's status in society as governments worldwide are placed under a legal and moral obligation to advance the cause of implementing the rights outlined in the Convention (United Nations Committee on the Rights of the Child, United Nations Children's Fund & Bernard van Leer Foundation, 2006). A major contributory factor to the influence of the UNCRC is its monitoring and international accountability functions. The UNCRC requires an active and deliberate decision by member states to ratify it. State parties are then required to submit a report to the UN Committee on the Rights of the Child (the monitoring and guiding body of the UNCRC) within two years of entry, and then every five years. One consequence of the UNCRC, and the advocacy work that surrounds it, is that slowly but surely children are beginning to emerge from their invisibility in society as both active citizens and social actors.

The UNCRC has been criticised by some for its ethnocentricity and has been viewed as an idealistic document (Freeman, 2000). Recognising that many children are engaged in exploitative work for extremely long hours and have no opportunities to play, Hart (1995) notes that the references to play in the UNCRC have very different implications for children in different countries. The use of the term 'rights' itself can also be problematic. As noted by Alderson (2005), the notion of rights today can be understood as 'Keep out! Don't interfere with me. I have the right to do whatever I like, as long as it doesn't harm anyone else'. Such a view applied to children can engender a 'nightmare vision of the selfish, unmanageable child, careless of parental love, and of responsibility, duty, loyalty or concern for others' (Alderson, 2005, p.134). In response, Alderson argues that the UNCRC involves concern for children's best interests, for public order, health and morals, and for parents' rights and duties. This implies an interdependent view of rights and responsibilities where rights are shared equally. She writes, 'Children's rights respect the inherent worth and dignity and the inalienable rights of all members of the human family. They promote social progress and better standards of life in larger freedoms that lay foundations for justice and peace in the world' (Alderson, 2005, p.134).

The UNCRC addresses children from birth to 18 years. However, arising from their experience of reviewing State parties' reports, the Committee on the Rights of the Child became concerned about the limited attention to babies and young children in general, and their dominant presentation as objects of care, protection and benevolence, rather than as rights-holders. A 'Day of General Discussion' devoted to early childhood was held on 17 September 2004, which led to the official adoption of General

Comment 7: 'Implementing Child Rights in Early Childhood' (2005) by the UN in January 2006. In the course of this process, which involved inputs from non-government organisations (NGOs) from all around the world (including from Ireland), many issues of concern relating to the understanding of and realisation of young children's rights were discussed and debated. Amongst the themes and constructs of the young child which emerged, are: firstly, young children's well-being, a good childhood, and what it means to have a good start in life; secondly, the notion of citizenship and democracy and how that is actualised in the lives of young children, and; thirdly, respect for diversity and equal opportunities. These constructs are becoming more prominent in framing ECEC in the twenty-first century at both global and local levels.

The role of ECEC in a 'good childhood'

At the Special Session of the United Nations General Assembly on Children in May 2002, 180 nations adopted the outcome document 'A World Fit for Children' in which they recognised that 'A world fit for children is one in which all children get the best possible start in life' (United Nations, 2002 cited by Engle (UNICEF), key note on General Discussion Day). Speaking to the assembled parties at the General Discussion day on implementing children's rights in early childhood, Patrice Engle elaborated by stating that:

> A good start in life means that each and every child, from infancy forward, has the right to live in a nurturing, caring and a safe environment that enables [the child] to survive and be physically health, mentally alert, emotionally secure, socially competent and able to learn (Engle, 2006).

The construct of what is 'good' goes beyond meeting basic needs for nurturance and shelter, coping and survival (Tuan, 1998).

Increasingly, the close human relationships that children establish are viewed as a highly significant feature of both a good start in life and a good childhood (Woodhead, 2006). Lothar Krappmann, a member of the UN Committee on the Rights of the Child, draws attention to the issue that young children must also be respected 'in their desire and strong determination to engage in activities that they themselves choose, invent, organise, regulate and enjoy'. In this regard, he noted that it was the intention of the Committee on the Rights of the Child to re-emphasise its responsibility to guarantee the rights of the young child 'to play and sing, to form groups and establish friendships, to engage in cultural activities and to explore the world on his or her own' (Krappmann, 2006, p.81). Thus a 'good' childhood also seems to 'speak to' children's instinctual sense of and eagerness to play, to be active, to explore (Kernan, 2006; Moss & Petrie, 2002; Sutton-Smith, 1997), to develop fantasies, to create works of art for their own enjoyment, to establish self-determined goals and self-evaluated proficiency (Krappmann, 2006), and to build friendships and culture and community (Hart, 1995).

Young children are in a relatively powerless position, which means they are dependent on others for the realisation of their rights of a good start in life and a good childhood. However, importantly, the predominant agenda for early childhood, advocated in contemporary discourse, is a positive one. Reflecting this, item 5 of General Comment No. 7 states that 'for the exercise of their rights, young children have particular requirements for physical nurturance, emotional care and sensitive guidance, as well as for time and space for social play, exploration and learning'. The question arises, however, as to how the notion of young children as rights-holders can be understood in terms of citizenship.

The UNCRC supports a child's right to grow into meaningful roles in society as full, democratic and participating citizens. For many young children worldwide, citizenship may be most relevant and most important in terms of the right to have their birth registered, and to have a birth certificate. Respecting children as citizens and as rights-holders also means viewing them as human beings with individual feelings, their own perspectives and their own distinct interests. Therefore young children are not only rights-holders in an abstract sense, but are accepted as active participants in the routine processes of daily life. Thus the onus is on responsible adults to listen and pay attention in order to capture the views and feelings the child expresses in verbal and non-verbal ways (Committee on the Rights of the Child, 2006). The voices of the youngest children can be viewed through their bodily actions and reactions, which are as trustworthy as the spoken word (Goldschmied & Selleck, 1996; Miller, 1997; Clark & Moss, 2001; Pramling Samuelsson, 2003). In this regard, Kjørholt, Moss & Clark, 2005 refer to the importance of valuing children's 'embodied expressions' of experience (p.176). An illustration of this in pedagogical practice is the ability of an early years practitioner to be attuned to babies' and toddlers' motivation to play. Often this requires adults to be able to 'read' the body language of a baby communicating his/her desire to play, to explore, or perhaps his/her need to feel secure. Clearly, play episodes occur throughout the day, may be embedded in routine care-giving and are often unplanned. A desire to play may be indicated *by looking out and pointing, crawling away, climbing, running, jumping, hiding*, whilst a need for security may be indicated by *searching, reaching up, hugging, clinging, approaching, following* (Manning-Morton & Thorp, 2003).

The notion of citizenship, understood as the right to participate actively in society, can also be closely associated with having access to space and time. One understanding of such participation that was explored by Kernan (2005) concerned the possibilities of children being visible and interacting outdoors in public community spaces with adults. The theoretical context for this study included: the explicit social and physical marginalisation of children, from the wider society by their location in particular places designed and supervised by adults for children including crèches, preschools, schools and playgrounds (Qvortrup *et al.*, 1995; James, Jenks, Prout, 1998); the idea that to be a child outside adult supervision, and visible on city streets amidst the wider society, for example, is to be 'out of place' (Fog Olwig & Gullov, 2003); the 'insularisation' of children's lives referred to earlier (Zeiher, 2001, 2003; Karsten, 2002); heightened fearfulness regarding children's vulnerability to risk and danger outdoors (Furedi, 2001; Thomas & Hocking, 2003; Valentine & McKendrick, 1997); the progressive reduction of green spaces; and the growing call to restore to children opportunities to make connections with the natural world outdoors (Kahn, 2005; Louv, 2005; Nabhan & Trimble, 1994; Rivkin, 1995; Stein, 2001).

The notion of citizenship and the young child in the context of ECEC has been extended by Dahlberg and Moss (2005) and Moss (2007) when they propose that ECEC settings can be understood as forums, spaces or sites for democratic political practice whereby children and adults can participate collectively in shaping decisions affecting themselves. Moss (2007) elaborates on such a 'paradigm' at a number of levels, including the institutional or 'nursery', the national or federal, the regional and the local. In this context, democracy is viewed both as a principle of government and a form of living together where there is a high value on sharing and exchanging perspectives and opinions and listening and dialogue (Moss, 2007). Such a way of viewing is more relevant than ever in Ireland – considering the potential roles and responsibilities of local government, county childcare committees and individual ECEC settings – in interpreting the new national frameworks for curriculum and quality. It also involves diverse challenges and roles for the early years practitioner, including being open to other possibilities and other perspectives, critical and reflective thinking and listening and sharing meaning of pedagogical work with others.

A diversity and equity approach to ECEC

One of the key features of contemporary societies, including Irish society, is that increasing numbers of young children are growing up in multicultural communities and in contexts marked by rapid social change. A diversity and equity approach to ECEC is based on the principles of inclusiveness (i.e. everyone belongs) and an appreciation of the origins of all (van Keulen, 2004). It requires paying attention to both commonalities and similarities within a group as well as acknowledging differences. A diversity and equity approach also places a high value on sharing and exchanging perspectives, opinions and listening. It is based on an understanding that all children can fulfil their common right to opportunities for active engagement with the social and physical environment, and ECEC settings have the responsibility of meeting this need and right in different ways, all of which work for and are meaningful for children (van Keulen, 2004).

A number of general key issues have been identified as warranting attention when reflecting on the meaning of such an approach in everyday practice in ECEC. Firstly, areas of 'difference', such as gender, ethnicity and socio-economic background, are fundamental parts of children's identity and have a significant impact on their experiential life, including their experience of play. Secondly, the period of the early years is when children are actively constructing images of themselves by comparing and contrasting themselves to others in their immediate everyday environments, such as the home and the ECEC setting. This process is also influenced by the views of significant adults in their lives as well as media images and children's own observations. Thirdly, all children are receptive to positive and negative behaviours, including misinformation and stereotyping of certain groups. Fourthly, the first time young children come across diversity is society is often in an ECEC setting. Therefore, it is important for early years practitioners to keep to the fore that diversity, equal opportunities and inclusion are not just minority issues, but issues that affect the majority also, making them important issues for all ECEC settings (McNaughton, 2003; Murray & O'Doherty, 2001; Siraj-Blatchford, 2004).

A number of researchers in the field have drawn attention to the power every adult has to affect (for good or bad) the self-identity, behaviour, actions, understandings and beliefs of the children they interact with (Derman-Sparks, 1989 Nutbrown, 1996; Siraj-Blatchford, 2004). Good practice in equal opportunities in ECEC indicates a proactive role for early years practitioners with respect to diversity and children's play and learning (Derman-Sparks, 1989; French, 2003; Nutbrown, 1996). This involves reflecting all children's backgrounds and abilities in the design, resourcing and images displayed in ECEC environments; actively supporting bi/multilingualism; being non-judgmental, and valuing a range of family forms, cultures and child-rearing practices; guiding children's developing attitudes and empowering them to stand up for themselves and others, and to feel proud of their own identity; supporting children's sense of belonging through their experiences of play and learning; carefully challenging and acting on discriminatory remarks and actions (Dickins & Denziloe, 1998; McNaughton, 2003; Murray & O'Doherty, 2001; Nutbrown, 1996). This places to the fore the moral and ethical dimensions of pedagogical work, which is often absent from discussions regarding the role of the early years practitioner (Brown & Freeman, 2001). When addressing moral, ethical or equity issues as they arise in planning for and evaluating provision in early childhood education, there is general agreement that a key starting point is how important it is for early years practitioners to reflect on their own personal values, as well as the professional values of the organisation or setting where they work. The policies of ECEC settings with regard to diversity and equal opportunities need deliberate and careful consideration, rather than persisting with a 'that's the way it's always been done' approach (Brown & Freeman, 2001). They also need ongoingmonitoring and regular evaluation (French, 2003). (The above section is taken from Kernan, 2007.)

SUMMARY

The everyday work life of early years practitioners encompasses a multitude of tasks and ways of relating and understanding. It can only be to the benefit of early years practitioners, and ultimately beneficial to young children and their families, if early years practitioners are able to understand and engage with many different perspectives and can draw on theory and knowledge from diverse disciplines and apply this knowledge in interrelated ways to practice. This chapter has highlighted a number of perspectives and ways of viewing that characterise early childhood pedagogy at the beginning of the twenty-first century. These include the importance of having a critical and reflective stance in everyday work with young children; the competing notions of structure and agency; interdependence between children and adults; the value of incorporating a philosophy of listening to young children and respecting their agency and natural learning strategies; the interactive and social nature of learning; the implications of viewing young children as citizens with rights and responsibilities, and a respect for diversity and equity approach in ECEC.

Point for reflection

Consider how viewing young children as citizens with rights and responsibilities can be incorporated into planning and everyday interactions in a manner that is meaningful to children, parents and communities within the local contexts within which you operate.

Chapter four

The Dynamics of Early Learning

INTRODUCTION

This chapter is the first of four linked chapters providing a theoretical and practical introduction to children's learning, learning contexts and practice. The chapter discusses current understandings of how young children learn and the dynamics of learning. In particular, it considers the relationship between development and learning and places the child centrally as an active participant in the social construction of knowledge and meaning. It explores the role of relationships and interactions in development, while recognising and elaborating on the importance of individual capabilities and dispositions. Throughout the chapter there is attention to the important role of context, the responsibilities of the adult and the contribution that children themselves play in their own development.

Development, learning and early education

Understanding how young children develop assists practitioners in considering how best to provide early childhood services. Over the last three decades there has been growing attention given to the relationship between education and development (Meadows, 1993; Siegler, 1996) and research data from a variety of disciplines has supported the theoretical position that '*human learning ... is participatory, proactive, communal, collaborative, and given over to constructing meanings rather than receiving them*' (Bruner, 1996, p. 84).

Learning to make sense of the world dominates early childhood education and characterises it as different from other levels of education. Even from very early on, the role of interactions in facilitating the 'meaning-making' process has been recognised (Dunn, 1987; Trevarthen, 1992; Rogoff, 1990; Wells, 1987). The child is learning to make sense of the world, and also learns by making sense. Adults play an important role in assisting children as this occurs and in directing their curiosity and questions in the way that is most appropriate to the context. '*As a teacher, you do not wait for readiness to happen; you foster or "scaffold" it by deepening the child's powers at the stage where you find him or her now*' (Bruner, 1996, p. 120). By giving this central place to the tasks of fostering and 'scaffolding' learning, Bruner is acknowledging the nurturing role of the adult in early education. This recognition of the active and social nature of early learning is key to refocusing attention on relationships within early education. However, while early educational research has provided data on what elements of settings and practice are most effective in terms of child outcome measures within early educational practice and provision, it does not provide answers as to why such elements are effective. The question remains: in what way does the more interactive, activity-based learning environment positively impact on child development when compared to other approaches, and how does this happen?

To gain insight into this question it is necessary to look at research from other disciplines such as developmental psychology. Parallel to the research in the early education field into settings, programmes/curricula, beliefs, practice and outcomes, there has been an expansion in child development research yielding a great deal of data which can inform and be informed by early educational research at both an academic and practice level. Overlap between and across different disciplines has the potential to be advantageous to all by creating new knowledge and understandings. By offering a sound psychological basis from which educational practice, curriculum development and educational assessment is developed, we can, through evaluation in practice, re-inform psychological research.

Reconceptualising development as learning

Early education researchers and practitioners must consider the mechanism of development and learning in young children if they are to understand why certain practices are more successful and appropriate than others. This is particularly important where investments are made to support early education as an intervention to counteract educational disadvantage. The direction of the relationship between learning and development is one that is often used to distinguish one major theoretical view of development from another (Berk & Winsler, 1995; French, 2007).

The most common perception is that learning and development are separate entities. In this view, development is the dominant process and learning refines and improves on structures that have already emerged. The twentieth-century theory driving this view is that of Piaget and his followers. Within education, teachers are seen not as instructing children, but as providing opportunities for them to discover knowledge for themselves. *'Teachers, of course, can guide them [children] by providing appropriate materials, but the essential thing is that in order for the child to understand something, he must construct it himself, he must reinvent it'* (Piaget, 1971, p.1). This rather strong statement about the individual nature of learning and the role of the teacher has been criticised as underestimating the importance of the social and the interpersonal in learning (Rogoff, 1990, 1998; Pellegrini & Bjorklund, 1998) and as downgrading the role of the teacher (Berk & Winsler, 1995; Donaldson, 1978; McGough, 2002).

A second viewpoint states that learning and development are identical; development results entirely from learning, which is defined as a measurable change in behaviour. In this model, the social environment provides the inputs necessary for learning and the passive child absorbs these inputs. Development is directed and driven by the environment, giving the manager of the environment – in educational settings the teacher – a great deal of organisational power and responsibility for the outcome. Such a view reflects the behaviourist or learning theorist position.

A third perspective is that learning leads to development; that is, learning plays a 'leading' role in development. It is a view that emerged from the work of Vygotsky who wrote that *'human learning presupposes a specific social nature and a process by which children grow into the intellectual life of those around them. ... learning which is oriented towards developmental levels that have already been reached are ineffective ... the only "good learning" is that which is in advance of development ... developmental processes do not coincide with learning processes. Rather, the developmental process lags behind the learning process; this sequence then results in zones of proximal development'* (1978, pp. 89–90). From this perspective the child and the socio-cultural environment interact to progress development.

Evans (1992) has suggested that there is a clear schism in developmental psychology whereby theories of development can be characterised as those who argue that it occurs as a result of naturalistic, indigenous growth, who is 'context-free', and those who see development as a result of 'environmental determination', which is 'context-sensitive'. Evans suggests that those educators who subscribe to a 'context-free' view accept the dominance of the universalist approach to child development, particularly the age and stage perspective, and will work on the basis that their approach applies to all children and that individual differences have a minor role. By contrast, those practitioners who subscribe to the power of impact of the environment on development, a 'context-sensitive' view, will argue for the management of that environment by adults for the achievement of specific outcomes. This management can be achieved by careful analysis of the learning situation. A contemporary view of development presents a more complex and dynamic scenario that lacks the clear and simple distinction between two poles proposed by Evans. Studies designed to capture the subtle dynamic patterns of teaching and learning in the early years have described development as a process which is 'context-sensitive' and influenced by the capabilities and past experiences of all involved.

Contemporary theorists continue to seek a greater understanding of the relationship between development and learning in terms that reflect the social nature of the individual (as proposed by Dewey and recognised, to a greater or lesser extent, by both Piaget and Vygotsky), and the powerful influence of the socio-cultural context within which learning and development occurs. This presents a new perspective, one that considers development and learning as the same, where the terms can be used interchangeably. Unlike the learning theorist perspective, which reduces development to learning as a measurable change in behaviour, this approach recognises that learning processes are as complex and dynamic as developmental processes. Rogoff (1997) subscribes to this view, which is supported by the socio-cultural theories that are emerging from discourse across disciplines. She points out that such theories stress the importance of the concept of *activity* to the analysis of development and refers to the work of Dewey (1916/1944), Lave & Wenger (1991), Rogoff (1990), Vygotsky (1978) and Wertsch (1991), who have all emphasised the role of participation in both face-to-face interactions and in indirect interpersonal arrangements of cultural activities.

Different theories of development shed light on different aspects of development with varying suggestions and challenges for educational principles and practices. Although system models attempting to explain development, such as that proposed by Bronfenbrenner, have been criticised for owing too much to a preoccupation with individualism and ignoring the power of inter-actions and discourse between parents, teachers and children in early education (Dahlberg, Moss & Pence, 1999; Lubeck, 1996; Penn, 1997), the value of a model such as the bio-ecological one is that it provides a framework that allows the enquirer to visualise the complex dynamics in different contexts. Furthermore, the con-struct of 'proximal processes' – as outlined by Bronfenbrenner and Morris (1998) – and their role as engines of development, are important. The quality of these 'proximal processes' is mediated by social interactions and this provides a link between the structure of development and the processes of development, which has implications for the practice of education. This proposal represents a rapprochement between the view of the child as 'structure' and the view of the child as 'agent'; neither is sufficient in and of itself. Against the backdrop of situational and contextual knowledge, the bio-ecological framework provides a model within which different educational approaches can be devised, drawing on a multitheoretical perspective.

Unlike earlier psychological research, aimed at imposing 'scientific' models of explanation on cognitive activity, contemporary research *'explores the child's own framework to understand better how he comes to the views that finally prove most useful ... such research provides the teacher with a far deeper and less con-descending sense of what she will encounter in the teaching and learning situation'* (Bruner, 1996, pp. 58–59). This focus on the importance of active participation of the child in context res-onates with parallel developments in respect of children's rights and children's visibility in the learning process in general. It challenges practitioners to consider what it means to facilitate such active participation, particularly in early education. Furthermore, it is important to realise that children cannot construct meaning through participation alone; there must be some appeal to concepts, some richness in content. This idea is further explored in chapter 5.

Development and learning in early education

One of the most influential theories applied to education from the realm of psychology has been that of Jean Piaget. The dominant position of the traditional Piagetian developmental model in early childhood education has given the impression of a child at a particular fixed stage of development progressing cumulatively through stages towards a developmental end point (Bloom, 1981; Bruner, 1996; Hayes, 1996, 2004). In addition to his characterisation of cognitive development as a staged process, Piaget also proposed the existence of cognitive structures or mechanisms (schema) through which experiences are represented and organised. His idea of cognitive development as occurring in stages and his concept of the child actively constructing knowledge – constructivism – have been singled out as Piaget's greatest contribution to education and research (Rogoff, 1990). Piaget also stressed that the learner is actively involved in the construction and reconstruction of schema through the dual processes of assimilation and accommodation, resulting from interactions with the environment. This view of the child as an architect of learning challenged practitioners to reconsider their role in education and move towards facilitating the formation of the mind rather than concentrating on furnishing it (deVries & Kohlberg, 1987).

Piaget has mistakenly been interpreted as considering only the individual at the expense of the environment and the social, and has been criticised as being too focused on the cognitive processes of the individual and neglectful of the wider social context as reflected in research on social situatedness (Wertsch, 1991) and situated learning (Lave and Wenger, 1991). This view is not entirely justified: as a biologist, he recognised and respected the role of the environment and the individual's need to adapt to it. However, his primary interest lay in how individuals adapted to their environments. He sought to present a structural theory of cognitive development to locate his work in a biological context. There is no doubt that his research focus was on individual development rather than the degree to which the social world contributes to that development. Influenced by Piaget, much research in both psychology and education emphasised and focused on the individual learner and their construction of reality. The dominant place that the staged theory has taken in education has, to a degree, acted as a barrier to considering the curriculum and practice implications of other more nuanced and sophisticated research emerging from within a systems framework which addresses some of the complexities of development and learning in context.

Within this wider view of development in context, Katz & Chard (1994) do not separate learning from development, but rather introduce the reader to two aspects of development that they consider as important. They point out that, traditionally, early childhood education has drawn heavily on descriptive studies of human development, with child study and child development being the key academic specialities of influence. Development is, they contend, most usefully considered as having two major dimensions: the normative and the dynamic.

The normative dimension has been a particularly dominant influence in early education in both curriculum development and recommendations for practice. It can also be observed in its application in classrooms where the stage of development of the child can be seen to follow a prescribed pattern – which in young children is to miss the point that they develop in a far messier and entangled way than the proposed linearity. The normative dimension of development addresses the question of what most children can and cannot do at a given age or stage and owes much to the work of Gesell in child study and Piaget in studies of cognitive development. 'When we say that an activity is developmentally appropriate, speak of grade level achievement or apply a Gesell-

type developmental measure, we are employing the normative dimension of the concept of development' (Katz & Chard, 1994, p.18).

A weakness in early educational literature and debate is that less attention is given to the dynamic dimension of development. It is the dynamic dimension that matters most when considering the development of young children as it provides a context for considering the way human beings change over time and with experience, the importance of delayed impact and the long-term cumulative effect of repeated or frequent experiences.

Sensitivity to both the normative and dynamic dimensions of development is critical in early education. The distinction between what young children can do and what they should do is especially serious in the early years because most children appear willing, if not eager, to do what is asked of them. This is a central issue of debate when considering curriculum and practice in the early years and one that has been recognised by a number of authors (Bloom, 1981; Bruce, 1987; Bruner, 1996; Elkind, 1988; Gardner, 1991).

Pellegrini & Bjorklund (1998) also identify two different approaches to considering development, and caution that when using the term 'development' one needs to be aware of which approach is meant. The first and most widespread model is that which characterises the child as an unfinished or incomplete adult and is best represented by the theories of both Piaget and Vygotsky. It is similar to the normative dimension discussed by Katz and Chard. The implication of this approach is that development proceeds along a specified path. Such a view has specific educational implications that have influenced various educationalists, whether coming from a Piagetian, Vygotskian or combined perspective (Athey, 1990; Hohman and Weikart, 1995; Shayer and Adey, 2002). In the US the influential early educational publication on Developmentally Appropriate Practice (DAP) (Bredekamp, 1987; Bredekamp and Copple, 1997) documents materials and activities that are identified as either 'appropriate' or 'inappropriate' for children at different ages and stages of their lives. The description (or as some see it, prescription) of 'appropriate' here is closely tied to the contribution these materials and activities make to the development of the child towardsoperational thinking and is based on the notion of development as a continuous progress toward adulthood. This view has generated a great deal of debate in early education literature and has informed an active research base on the topic of curriculum and practice (Canella, 1998; Dahlberg *et al.*, 1999; Lambert & Clyde, 2000; Lubeck, 1996).

The second model of development identified by Pellegrini and Bjorklund (1998) is that which views each developmental period as being valuable for that specific time. In this model, 'childish' behaviours are seen as adaptive to the period and not regarded as imperfect but rather as important responses to the 'niche' of childhood. '*The idea that a behaviour, such as play, has immediate rather than deferred benefits is consistent with the view that development is an adaptation to the specific demands of a niche, such as childhood. The important point to stress here is that behaviour may serve different functions at different periods of development*' (p. 17). In other words, different behaviours may serve present and future functions at one and the same time. In some cases there is continuity of similar behaviours over time which they refer to as *homotypic continuity* (where the form of behaviour is the same across time). There are many examples and they instance the observations of physically active infants also recorded as active during their preschool years. *Heterotypic continuity*, on the other hand, is more difficult to track. It refers to a developmental link across time between two dissimilar behaviours. They give as an example the ability to engage in make-believe play at age three years related to word-reading at age five. They contend that make-believe play and word-reading involve different response modes, but are theoretically related to the extent that they both involve manipulation of symbolic representation. The essence of 'being developmental' is, through observation, to identify and track changes in individual children and value the moment for its immediate developmental contribution whilst acknowledging – but not overemphasising – its potential in respect of later development.

If one considers that development is a continuous, linear process, which is the more traditional view, then disturbances in the early processes will be seen to have a special significance with important, and sometimes irreversible, effects. On the other hand, viewing development as a dynamic and discontinuous process, or as the 'to-ing and fro-ing' process proposed by Lambert and Clyde (2000), allows one to view behaviour and development in early childhood as adaptive to the demands of the niche of childhood. Such a perspective to development and context provides an alternative view of 'appropriate' to that proposed by Bredekamp & Copple (1997). From this perspective 'appropriate' should be seen to refer to the role of individuals, materials and activities in meeting the immediate and particular needs of childhood rather than as a preparation for the next stage of development or for adulthood. This view of developmentally appropriate practice is compatible with that discussed by Dahlberg *et al.* (1999) and Penn (1997), who are critical of the dominance of the DAP perspective in debates within early education. They propose an approach to early education that is not tied to the age and stage of development of the child but rather linked to the socio-cultural context of development for the child in the present. Such an approach, they argue, is exemplified by the practices at Reggio Emilia in Italy and in the Te Whariki early years curriculum of New Zealand where pedagogy is directed by the connections, interactions and relationships between children and the wider world – social, physical and emotional – rather than by prescribed expectations of developmental outcome (New Zealand, 1996; Edwards, Gandini & Forman, 1995).

The role of relationships and interactions in development

Bruner (1996) suggests that if pedagogy is to empower humans beyond their potential, it must transmit the tools (including, but not only, the symbolic tools) appropriate to the society. These tools empower children to explore their own way of thinking and problem-solving. To assist this Bruner stresses the importance of intense interactions in language-rich environments. Such interactions are similar to the proximal processes proposed by Bronfenbrenner and his colleagues as the basis from which to consider the question of why interactions are so important to development (Bronfenbrenner & Morris, 1998).

It is beyond the scope of this chapter to review the extensive data emerging from neuropsychological, brain and psychological research that support the importance of interactions to development. However, authors such as Greenfield (2000) and Shore (1997) give useful reviews of research findings from various theoretical stances which underpin the critical importance of early interactions to the development and learning of young children. Development is a process of continuous change that is self-maintaining, self-restoring and self-regulating (Bronson, 2001; Gaussen, 2002; Kuhn, 1997). Early brain research indicates that the brain is only partially mature at birth and continues to develop over the first years of life (Karmiloff-Smith, 1992; Shore, 1997). This makes it immediately susceptible to the ongoing influence of experiences of all types. Changes in development result from reciprocal transactions of the biologically maturing child with the social, physical and cultural environment (Bronfenbrenner, 1995) and the quality of interactions impacts on development (Trevarthen, 1992). Culture is an organising influence in development (Bruner, 1996; Cole, 1996; Vygotsky, 1978) and the learning context is important. Studies indicate that 'meaning-making' activity is enhanced by quality interactions. Results from observation of infant-caregiver interactions highlights the importance of joint attention to objects and events in assisting infants to come to recognise meaning-making and intention on the part of the other (Dunn, 1987). Such data suggests that the shared construction of knowledge does not simply involve a cumulative effect of multiple, individual contributions, but represents a stronger view of learning and the importance of the act of interacting, of shared meanings growing out of participation in shared activity. Such insights into development, among others, have led to increased attention from economists on why we should invest in early education (Heckman, 2000). While research in neuroscience is providing exciting data about early brain development and the importance of interactions with people and objects, there is, as yet, no clear link between results from such research and implications for teaching and learning in practice. However, a review of such research by Blakemore and Frith (2000) did conclude that *there is no biological necessity to rush and put the start of teaching earlier and earlier. Rather, late starts might be reconsidered as perfectly in tune with findings from ... brain research'* (p. 4). This statement challenges those involved in early education to consider carefully how we create positive learning opportunities for young children and avoid 'schoolification' (Bennett, 2005).

Many research studies have investigated how interactions impact on child development. Findings provide us with rich and powerful evidence about why they are important to how children learn, the nature of learning and the ways in which early experiences shape the patterns of progress, achievement and fulfilment throughout an individual's life. This research highlights the importance of developing learning dispositions (Katz, 1995; Perkins *et al.* 1993; Carr, 2002; Lambert & Clyde, 2000); encouraging a mastery or learning orientation (Ames, 1992; Dweck & Leggett, 1988; Heyman, G., Dweck, C. S. and Cain, K. 1992); promoting metacognitive skills (Kuhn, 1995, 1997, 1999; Shayer & Adey, 2002); developing cognitive and social self-regulation (Bronson, 2001); providing for multiple intelligences (Gardner, 1991, 1993); and fostering engaged involvement and emotional well-being (Goleman, 1996; Laevers, 1994, 2002). The picture emerging is one of quality early education settings as dynamic environments rich in interactions and communication where learning and development occurs in a complex, dynamic and shared context and not simply as a result of individual differences in ability or a specific pedagogy.

The move from considering education as a process of transmission towards one of construction has been well argued and, in most Western early educational literature, one sees acknowledgement of the need to consider both the individual and the socio-cultural context when evaluating learning. However, the debate has moved beyond this again towards the notion, articulated by Rogoff (1990, 1997), Kuhn (1992, 1995) and others, of education as dynamic transformation. Interactions are seen as the locus and carriers of learning, mediating mechanisms for development (Packer, 1993), and the role of the practitioner is key. The mechanisms to allow this conceptualisation have begun to emerge from certain areas of child development research and are explored below.

The role of the zone of proximal development and scaffolding

A metaphor widely used in the literature to describe effective teaching/learning interactions is that of 'scaffolding'. The term is often used to describe the Vygotskian concept of Zone of Proximal Development (ZPD), although the two concepts developed independently of each other. In his writings on educational implications, Vygotsky defines ZPD as *'the distance between the child's actual level of development as a measure of their independent behaviour and his or her potential development level in a social context with adult or peer guidance or collaboration... the ZPD defines those functions that have not yet matured but are in the process of maturation, functions that will mature tomorrow but are currently in an embryonic state'* (p.86). The emphasis is on the learner as a maturing organism who is passive in the role of development but who can be guided to the next developmental stage by the informed adult. Vygotsky argued that the ZPD furnishes psychologists and educators with a mechanism for cultivating higher-order cognitive functions, a tool through which the internal course of development can be understood.

Wood, Bruner & Ross (1976) introduced the idea of adults scaffolding learning to both structure and extend children's activities and learning. Although they did not draw explicitly on the work of Vygotsky and his notion of ZPD when formulating their construct of scaffolding, there are clear parallels between the two ideas and they are often used interchangeably. The scaffolding metaphor captures the Piagetian notion of the child as a constructor of knowledge and the construction is supported, or scaffolded, by the social environment within which such construction is occurring. Generally the adult is considered as the scaffold to the child's development. Bruner (1996) has identified the goals of adult–child scaffolding as joint problem-solving, intersubjectivity, warmth/responsiveness and promoting self-regulation. This image, though suggestive of supportive interaction, continues to emphasise the adult-to-child nature of scaffolding and is reminiscent of the approach implied in the original proposals on ZPD. Such a description of scaffolding masks the active contribution of the child and reduces their role to that of a mere recipient of the adult's didactic efforts. Such a view is disingenuous as it perpetuates the vision of the child as active in learning only by reference to the construction of knowledge in response to the adult.

Both ZPD and scaffolding have been criticised as presenting too passive a view of the child and too instructional a role for the expert. The direction of the interactions, from the adult/expert to the novice/learner, is considered unidirectional and insufficiently sensitive to the important role of the process of the interaction itself within the scaffold metaphor or the ZPD space. Cullen (2001) notes that the argument that early studies of ZPD and scaffolding located the learner as passive began to be addressed in the work of Rogoff (1990; Rogoff, Mosier, Mistry & Goncu, 1993) and Valsiner (1988, 1997). Both Rogoff and Valsiner moved from the cognitive constructivist idea of Piagetian scholars and the social constructivist idea of Vygotskian scholars to a view of co-construction of knowledge where the concept of 'intersubjectivity' and joint activity becomes central.

Limitations of the zone of proximal development and scaffolding

The uncritical acceptance of the scaffolding metaphor in early education discussion and practice has been criticised by Lambert and Clyde (2000). They acknowledge the potential of scaffolding as a concept, but make a case for reconsidering it from the contextualised perspective specific to early education rather than *'passively accepting interpretations from within the discipline of psychology, or other domains of knowledge, that may not be contextualised to the needs of younger children'* (p. 59). Sylva (1997) has argued that educators often want simple solutions to resolve complex problems and when these simple solutions don't work they abandon them. She suggests that teachers wanted and found a slogan in the notion of scaffolding but that too simplistic an interpretation of the power of scaffolding led to its failure in the reality of current class sizes and curricular demands.

Contemporary authors, including Bruner (1996), have considered the possibility of extending the idea of scaffolding to make it more powerful and effective as a tool in education. More attention needs to be given to the active role of the child in the scaffolding process and to the emotional aspect of relationships between the child and others as, historically, too much attention has been given to the mode of adult–child interchange where the adult engages in explicitly didactic instruction, thereby reducing the child to a passive recipient. This could be done by allowing for the child to be viewed as the 'experienced other'. Bickhard (1992) contends that the usual conception of scaffolding is limited in that it is seen as providing what the child lacks in order to make possible performance that might otherwise not emerge. He proposes an extension of the original notion of scaffolding to include different types of scaffolding at different levels of influence, including child–child scaffolding. His refinement of the mechanism is intended to extend the power of scaffolding in learning, and his suggestion that the locus of development is the system engaged in the interactions of scaffolding itself does give it a potentially powerful role. Through scaffolding the child not only accomplishes something he or she might not have otherwise accomplished (a process Bickhard calls 'recursive variation'), but is also supported by the process to develop 'enabling' competencies (which he calls 'metarecursive variations'). These 'enabling' competencies may be related to procedures or strategies other than the content of the scaffolded experience. Thus, through scaffolding the child develops content knowledge and skills, but also procedural knowledge, which assists in the development towards self-regulating scaffolding and the construction of new knowledge. In addition to extending the view of the process of scaffolding, Bickhard also sees potential for different forms of scaffolding, including the 'institutional scaffolding' provided by schools, youth clubs, sporting groups, and 'environmental scaffolding' located in the learning environment, including expectations, values and beliefs. Interestingly, work on peer collaboration at secondary school, within the scaffolding framework, has been reported by Shayer and his colleagues (2002).

This more complex view of scaffolding in early education should be set against the theoretical framework where development and learning are recognised as a complex, dynamic process which is multidirectional and influenced by socio-cultural contexts (Cole, 1996; Rogoff, 1990; Kuhn, 1995, 1999; Winegar & Valsiner, 1992). To capture this dynamic concept, Lambert and Clyde (2000) propose the notion of 'reciprocal scaffolding' as more in line with current thinking about young children's learning. They define reciprocal scaffolding as the situational scaffolding used to co-construct higher levels of understanding or ability with a learner. An ultimate aim of reciprocal scaffolding in early education is development towards degrees of self-scaffolding. Reciprocal scaffolding includes the attachment relationship between the child and adult (emotional aspect), the physical environment (materials support) and the social ethos (social supports) (2000, p. 59).

Individual capabilities and dispositions

Children are learning all the time. Individual learning power, or cognitive functioning, has two dimensions: *capabilities* (the skills and strategies), and *dispositions* (the tendencies to learn and learn from learning) (Resnick & Klopfer, 1989). Dispositions are an integral part of the individual child and can be identified through observing children's choices, decisions and actions. To develop and function, they require a balance between the inclination of the learner and the goals of knowledge, skills and abilities to be learned. This developmental view of dispositional learning is in keeping with our current understanding of the complex and dynamic nature of learning and is the reason that consideration must be explicitly given to the fostering of learning dispositions in early education. It suggests an active role for the adult and the learning environment in the development of learning dispositions as well as in the teaching of skills and knowledge.

Conceptions about early learning in traditional early childhood curricula include the assumption that learning in early childhood is a preparation for future learning and is about '*acquiring the early rungs of a hierarchy of defined knowledge and skill, a process that begins the climb up the ladder to grown-up ways of thinking and learning*' (Carr, 1998, p.1). Such assumptions consolidate the view of the learner as an individual and learning as furniture of the mind. New conceptions about the curriculum recognise that it is in early childhood that children get their first messages about themselves, about what it is to be a learner, and about the expectations and constraints that an environment can place on this. David (1990) has expressed concern that early educators, while attending to the development of literacy and numeracy skills, may, in fact, underestimate the cognitive abilities of young children. As has been illustrated, research from child development suggests that young children are capable of developing higher-order thinking skills. Resnick (1987) draws a distinction between the development of higher-order thinking and the cultivation of dispositions to apply higher-order thinking. Cultivating the disposition to apply higher-order thinking challenges educators in early education to consider how best to nurture the development and application of these skills.

As the development of skills and knowledge is seen as the aim of traditional education, focusing on ability, so dispositional development is the aim of education focusing on the social, emotional or affective aspect. There is, in fact, no compelling evidence that early introduction to academic work guarantees success in school in the long term. On the contrary, there is reason to believe that, because of the dynamic nature of development, the cumulative effects of early introduction may inhibit or work against development of desirable disposition. So, for instance, although an early focus on the development of skills associated with academic work might result in young children with strong literacy and numeracy skills, the experience may also inhibit the development of the dispositions to become readers, scientists and appliers of mathematics. Katz (1993) notes that there is a significant and important difference between being able to read and being disposed to read, being able to listen and having a disposition to listen. Both are interdependent; learning a skill or developing the ability may tend to make one more inclined to engage in that skill or ability and, conversely, the disposition to learn about something tends to lead to greater engagement and associated success. However, researchers on this topic caution that knowledge and skills developed do not necessarily transfer from one context to the next. For instance, in her research Carr (1997) found that risk-taking and collaborative abilities revealed in socio-dramatic play were not necessarily transferred over to more school-like construction activities. She also notes that dispositions depend on context and are sensitive to occasion. For instance, there are times when it is appropriate to persist at a task and times when it may be inappropriate; a child may assume that to persist at something is inappropriate if a task is considered, for instance, as gendered; she instances the example of woodwork classes, where girls are less likely than boys to persist. Similarly, dispositions might never develop if the opportunities are not presented. It is important to consider fostering dispositions as well as capabilities when seeking to understand the complex process of cognition and adjust curricular aims and pedagogical practice in early education to facilitate the transfer of such learning to new learning contexts.

Since the mid-1980s the term 'disposition' has begun to appear with greater frequency in literature about children's learning (Katz, 1985; Resnick, 1987; Katz & Chard, 1994; Perkins *et al.*, 1993). Katz (1993) lists seven reasons for including the development of dispositions as a goal in early education (p. 11–12):

1. The acquisition of knowledge and skills alone does not guarantee that they will be used and applied.
2. Dispositional considerations are important because the instructional process by which some knowledge and skills are acquired may damage or undermine the disposition to use them.
3. Some dispositions relevant to education, such as the disposition to investigate, may be thought of as inborn. When children's experiences are supported to manifest dispositions they become robust; without such supports they are likely to weaken or disappear.
4. The process of selecting curricula and teaching strategies

should include consideration of how desirable dispositions can be strengthened and how undesirable dispositions can be weakened.

5.   On the basis of evidence accumulated from research on mastery *versus* performance motivation, it seems reasonable to suggest that there is an optimum amount of positive feedback for young children above which children may become preoccupied with their performance and the judgment of others rather than involvement in the task.

6.   Dispositions must be included in the evaluation and assessment of an educational programme.

7.   Dispositions are not likely to be acquired through didactic processes, but are more likely to develop in young children as they experience being around people who exhibit them. Therefore, teachers and parents should become aware of what dispositions can be seen in them by the children for whom they are responsible.

This list affords a useful basis from which researchers and practitioners can study the development and influence of learning dispositions in young children and their education.

Considerable work on dispositions in an early educational context is emerging from New Zealand, where the concept has become a core element of their early education curriculum (1996). In particular, the concept of learning dispositions in early education has been critically refined and conceptually and operationally clarified by the work of Carr (1997; 1998; 2001a; 2001b). Her work has extended the idea of dispositions to the field of early learning and also focuses on the distinction between capabilities and dispositions. She has distinguished learning dispositions from thinking dispositions – regarding thinking as an element of learning – and has defined learning dispositions in early education as *'participation repertoires from which a learner recognises, selects, edits, responds, searches for and constructs learning opportunities'* (2000b, p. 1).

Drawing on her analysis of the New Zealand early education curriculum, *Te Whariki,* Carr identifies six key learning dispositions: courage, curiosity, playfulness, perseverance, confidence and responsibility. She characterises learning dispositions as 'being ready, willing and able' to learn. She believes such dispositions can be fostered through appropriate pedagogy (2001b). This characterisation of a good learner draws on the work of Claxton (1990) who wrote that '*it can be strongly argued that schools' major responsibility must be to help young people become ready, willing and able to cope with change successfully: that is, to be powerful and effective learners*' (p. 164). Carr views *being ready* as seeing oneself as a learner; it is about having a strong personal identity of self as a learner. Much of the work of Dweck and her colleagues centres around how this disposition develops as an adaptive 'learning orientation' (becoming, as Bronfenbrenner outlines (Bronfenbrenner & Morris, 1998), a generative disposition) as opposed to its developing as a non-adaptive 'performance orientation' (becoming a disruptive (Bronfenbrenner) or damaged (Katz) disposition). *Being ready* to learn is a characteristic of individual children that can be cultivated by the teacher and the environment. It is that element of education which confirms and endorses children as participating learners in the educational process, or not. *Being willing*, on the other hand, is more about process than a characteristic. It is a transactional process between the learner and the environment for which the teacher has considerable responsibility. *Being willing* is recognising that this place is (or is not) a place for learning. *Being able* is having the abilities and funds of knowledge that will contribute to the relevant actions associated with being a participant learner, owing much to opportunity and experience.

The concept of learning disposition and its relevance to early education in terms of children being ready, willing and able is valuable because it allows the teacher to focus on the individual child as unique, link the individuality of the child with contextually desirable aspects of learning, and create an early childhood curriculum that empowers the child towards present learning and future school and life success. A critical curriculum for the early years should include 'learning goals' as a key outcome; it will need deliberate nurturing by adults to establish a learning climate in which stereotypes are questioned, new challenges are tackled and where it is standard practice to risk being wrong. Carr suggests that an outcome for early education is the development of adaptive learners who can effectively coordinate performance and learning goals, balancing curriculum aims of belonging and exploration. Her research supports the notion that the basis of learning or performance goals appears to be socio-culturally and historically linked to social identity. Learning-orientated children strive to increase their competence, to understand or master something, to attempt hard tasks and persist despite failure or setback. Performance-orientated children, on the other hand, strive to gain favourable judgments and avoid negative judgment of their competence. They are anxious to appear competent to the extent that they avoid harder tasks where the outcome is uncertain. These characteristics have been found in children as young as four or five years of age (Smiley & Dweck, 1994).

Despite the recognition that early education must balance attention between developing the capacities and the dispositions of the learner and the encouraging data emerging from research into fostering and assessing learning dispositions, there are difficulties with the concept of disposition itself. To begin with, it is difficult to define (Carr, 1998; Campbell, 1999). It has been used to describe pro-social qualities such as cooperative disposition, or accepting disposition (Katz, 1995a), thinking qualities (Perkins *et al.*, 1993; New Zealand, 1996) and learning qualities (Carr, 1998, 2001b). Campbell (1999) calls for desirable dispositions to be defined and described clearly. She goes on to argue that the case for the existence of universal dispositions has yet to be made and challenges researchers to find a way of considering dispositions within the frame of a child's thinking, inclinations, goals, knowledge, skills and abilities to provide concrete tools for developing a child's desirable dispositions within early educational practice. Carr (1998, 2001b) provides a thorough conceptualisation of learning dispositions in early education which goes some way to meeting these demands.

Implications for early childhood education and care

The argument then is that including a consideration of interactions in early educational pedagogy is necessary and valid given the role that interactions (their quality, bidirectionality and content) play in facilitating the development of thinking skills (cognitive and metacognitive) and affective skills (disposition); that is their role in developing knowledge and skills, knowledge about knowledge and the inclination and readiness to apply knowledge.

Historically in early education policy and research, attention was focused on the concept of intelligence, largely due to the use of the IQ as a child outcome measure in evaluation studies. The concept of intelligence is both political and academic (Herrenstein & Murray, 1994; Pinker, 2002). It is a concept that has polarised thinkers and politicians, has influenced policy in education to no small degree, and continues to generate debate and discussion. It is a psychological construct that is often studied in isolation from the context in which it is expressed, which is at odds with our current understanding of development in general. One of the contemporary debates in the study of cognition concerns the degree to which there exists a general intellectual skill as opposed to specific skills which may be domain or discipline bound (Glaser, 1984) or context specific (Ceci 1990; Lave and Wenger, 1991). This distinction has been characterised by Dweck and her colleagues as an 'entity' view of intelligence versus an 'incremental' view (Dweck & Bempechat, 1980) and has been found to influence both children and teachers in their approaches to learning (this is discussed in Chapter 5). Theorists like Gardner (1993; 1999) and Sternberg (1998) argue that characterising intelligence as a general capacity is too limiting. They have both put forward alternative, more inclusive theories of intelligence. Gardner has proposed the notion of multiple intelligences and Sternberg suggests that intelligence is best considered an *'ability to balance the need to adapt, to shape and select environments in order to attain success ... within one's socio-cultural context'* (1998, p. 438).

This more flexible conceptualisation of the process underlying intelligent action would result in consideration of the detail of context as an influencing element in teaching and learning which, although well known since the seminal work of Donaldson (1978) on understanding young children's thinking, appears to have had limited impact. Contemporary studies of development move beyond the individual to consider the interactive nature of development, the role of the individual and the environment as a transactional unit, each with the potential to transform the other. The shift in conceptualising intelligence from biological adaptation towards social construction requires some redefinition to include *'not just the cognitive skills and forms of knowledge that have classically been considered the essence of intelligence, but also a cluster of social performances such as asking questions, striving to master new problems and seeking help in problem-solving'* (Resnick & Nelson-Le Gall, 1997 p. 145).

But can children develop such skills? Are they capable of higher-order thinking and of exhibiting metacognitive skills? Various authors, from different perspectives, have argued that abstract thinking is no less common in young children than concrete thinking and have emphasised the role of dialogue in facilitating its manifestation and development (Bruner, 1996; Egan, 1997; Resnick, 1987). This emphasis on dialogue is a central feature of Vygotsky's approach to instruction within the ZPD. Some authors suggest that 'poor' metacognitive skills may actually be adaptive, pointing out that young children's optimistic, and often unrealistic opinions of their own abilities may foster their developing sense of self-efficacy. '*If they knew how poorly they did on most tasks, young children might be discouraged and quit*' (Pellegrini & Bjorklund, 1998, p. 140). This view of the adaptive function of certain 'immature' behaviours having a survival value in the naive credulity of young children would be characterised as maladaptive in later life. Egan contends that higher-order functions, such as metacognition, begin with social relations, in interactions with others, where the social nature of people comes to be their psychological nature. Such a view recognises the young, social child as capable of reasoning, by and while making sense of the world, and presents the child as capable of higher-order functions such as thinking about thinking, connecting ideas through reflection or 'going meta' (Bruner, 1996, p. 57). This demands a considered and informed approach to practice.

One of the benefits of developing metacognitive skills is that it assists in the development of cognitive self-regulation. Bronson (2001) argues that one of the tasks of childhood is to develop the ability to regulate cognitive functioning, to exercise conscious control over attention and memory processes. Accumulating research evidence suggests that, to some extent, children spontaneously develop these capacities, but it also suggests that the environment can assist or disrupt their development. Language and a language-rich environment can assist young children in the development of their self-regulatory skills.

Preschool children (three–five year olds) are learning how to learn and how to solve problems. They are developing strategies for cooperative and positive social interactions. As they develop, their behaviour sheds light on their developing capabilities. Experience in attempting to carry out cognitive tasks successfully is influenced by the environment and the responsiveness of those in the environment. As a guide to practice, Bronson (2001) notes that '*environments that nurture self-regulation are orderly and consistent enough for children to understand the requirements for successful independent functioning within them. They provide appropriate ground rules for action that allow children to carry out a variety of activities, alone or with peers, without the need for constant adult control. The materials and activities in these environments are also designed to interest and challenge children and to support self-regulated activities'* (p. 220).

Behaviours that assist children in achieving their potential include the ability to become absorbed and to concentrate; a willingness to try the new; a facility to listen to themselves as well as others; an honesty that allows them to be individual; a readiness to assume responsibility; the ability to work hard and persevere. Also important to this process is the sense of belonging that assists in the development of well-being (Laevers, 2002). Prioritising emotional and social development, particularly in early education, can assist the children in their overall development.

SUMMARY

The dominant influence of the Piagetian theory of cognitive development in early educational research and practice is being challenged by a more complex, socio-cultural approach to understanding young children's learning in context, taking account of the active role they play in this learning. Early educational initiatives, particularly for children from three to six years of age, have given rise to a rich body of research which has identified many of the characteristics of quality early education. Child development is enhanced, for instance, in classrooms that are well organised and child-focused and where teachers play an active, facilitative role rather than a didactic one. High-quality learning environments are those where teachers interact with children in a responsive and informative way, encouraging verbal and social interactions, and where teachers have high expectations of children. Key features of high-quality early education include: classrooms with fewer children, oppor-tunities for child-to-child interactions and teachers with a high level of appropriate training who give specific and responsive attention to individual children and are reflective and flexible in their planning and practice.

The development of individual children is most usefully character-ised in both normative and dynamic terms. An understanding of normative development has been found useful in guiding curriculum planning but, in day-to-day early educational practice, research suggests that it is the dynamic dimension of development that is most important for the individual child and teacher. The opportunity for positive interactions between children and their environment – the people, materials and ideas – has also been identified as a crucial element influencing positive development. Current research from developmental psychology indicates that it is not simply the opportunity for interactions but the actual process itself that is important. In particular, research is highlighting the value of dynamic, bidirectional social interactions as crucial to early development. Bidirectional, transformational interactions in stable learning environments are important because they facilitate development of skills, knowledge and dispositions by helping children to explain their ideas to others, negotiate and argue a point and clarify their thinking, thus refining their social, cognitive and metacognitive skills.

Points for reflection

This chapter explores how young children learn and develop and highlights the key role of the adult in creating rich learning opportunities. A distinction is drawn between normative and dynamic development and the argument is made that the adult role in facilitating dynamic development is key to positive early educational experiences. Drawing on your own history of working with young children, reflect on their behaviour, interactions and language and on your responses. Recognising children's own contribution through their unique experiences, capabilities and dispositions, consider how your practice facilitates the development of positive learning dispositions. In particular, review how one can maximise curricular and pedagogical opportunities to this end.

Chapter five

From Vision to Curriculum

INTRODUCTION

Building on our understanding of how young children learn, this chapter reviews different curricular approaches used in early education. The very word curriculum can create difficulties when considering early education and, to address this, the chapter describes a range of different curricular approaches found in Ireland, New Zealand, Italy and elsewhere. In reviewing the various approaches – each influenced by different political and theoretical backgrounds – this chapter explores the underlying principles and values informing them. The value of a rich, responsive and emergent curriculum is discussed and the role and importance of play within such a curricular approach is considered.

In search of effective models of early education

While some academics and researchers were investigating the competencies of young children in areas such as metacognition and theory of mind, others were questioning the dominant focus on skills and knowledge as goals for early education. At its most polarised, one of the major questions in the debate centres around whether it is more beneficial for children if programmes follow the traditional model of education found at primary level (large group, teacher-directed, formal instruction in subject domains) or if they should focus on education through small-group, child-initiated, informal, activity-based models. Studies indicate that there may be advantages and disadvantages to both approaches. Schweinhart & Weikart (1997), writing about models of early intervention, note that the teacher-directed method seems to discourage social and emotional development, learning dispositions and creativity in children, while an exclusively child-initiated, activity-based model may be insufficient to assist general academic development. Longitudinal research, primarily from the United States, supports the principle that activity-based programmes that respect children as active participants in the early educational process yield sustainable benefits in terms of academic and social success in later life, with measurable effects on school achievement and adolescent and adult adjustment. Marcon (1999), in her extensive review of three different models of early education, found that the academically oriented programme showed a less beneficial effect on young inner-city children than the 'mixed' programme, where traditional academic methods were balanced by more play-based, active learning. However, this 'mixed' model did not yield as positive a result as the fully committed activity-based programme. The longitudinal element of her research suggests that the trajectory of difference across these different models, favouring the latter, grows as the children progress through school. Other studies showing similar results include the High/Scope Perry Preschool Project (Schweinhart, Barnes & Weikart, 1993; Schweinhart and Weikart, 1997) and the Carolina Abecedarian Project (Ramey & Ramey, 1998; Ramey, Campbell, Burchinal, Skinner, Gradner & Ramey, 2000). The largest UK study, the Effective Provision of Preschool Education (EPPE) project, is a longitudinal study of the impact of early childhood experiences across the age range 3–7 years. Unlike the studies reported from the US, the EPPE project conducted a national sample of children and settings and did not confine itself to centre-based intervention projects. Within its overall sample there was a sufficient sample of settings catering for poorer children to allow analysis on the differential impact of settings across socio-economic groups. Findings reflect those of similar studies and offer some additional insights (Sylva *et al.*, 2004). They found that early educational experiences did have a positive effect on child outcomes for all children, although they caution that children with extensive experience of group care under the age of two showed slightly higher levels of anti-social behaviour. The explanation for this may be related to the quality of settings and the user population. Overall, disadvantaged children, and boys in particular, benefit significantly from good quality preschool. In addition they found that the quality of the home learning environment (HLE) is more important for intellectual and social development than parental occupation, education or income. In their interpretation of this finding, the authors note that what the parents *do* seems to be more important than who the parents *are* (Sylva *et al.*, 2004).

There are limitations to the extent one can apply these findings directly to curriculum development and there is no single programme or approach that works for all children in all settings. The methods used in evaluative studies, the questions asked by the researchers and the outcome measures chosen to evaluate effectiveness vary from study to study, making direct comparisons difficult. Determining which approach to early education is appropriate in any given situation will depend on the context, values, goals and implementation of different programmes. Is there a common thread evident in the different successful programmes, a principle or goal common to them all?

In reviewing possible explanations for the successes attributed to different models, Egertson (2003) observed that, in general, successful programmes are well planned and staff are well trained and supported in their work. All recognise the importance of quality early education for later school success. In particular, all have a strong commitment to developing the affective dimension of learning. This reflects the views expressed by Rutter (1985) and Ball (1994) and others who concluded that the most important learning in early education has to do with the 'soft' and difficult-to-measure aspects of development, such as aspirations, social skills, motivation and learner confidence. Research evidence suggests that this strong emphasis on the affective dimensions of learning (focusing on the development of aspirations, task commitment, social skills and feelings of efficacy) positively influences children's academic cognitive development (content knowledge and academic skills). This approach yields foundational short-term benefits and sustainable long-term benefits across social and educational dimensions. There is no convincing evidence from the research that this process is commutative, that a similar emphasis on the academic dimension of cognitive development positively influences the affective dimension in children. This conclusion goes beyond the idea of a simple interrelatedness between academic and affective dimensions of development and proposes a strong line of influence in one direction rather than the other. The implications of this interpretation suggest that, rather than attempting to provide a balanced or mixed approach to guiding academic and affective skills development in young children, it would be more productive to foreground the social/emotional, or affective, dimension of development in early education. Some work to this effect is already underway in New Zealand (New Zealand, 1996), Italy, in the Reggio Emilia region in particular (Edwards *et al.*, 1995; Rinaldi, 1995) and, to a lesser extent, in the UK (OECD, 2006). Such a shift in focus requires rethinking the early years curriculum to include a reformulation of the goals of early education, a review of the role of the adult and the child in the learning environment and a re-consideration of assessment processes. Grounds for supporting this refocus on the affective dimension of learning in young children can be found in our understanding of how young children learn, particularly the results of research into motivation and dispositions that have emerged from child development research.

What is an early years curriculum?

Defining what exactly a curriculum is in early education is quite difficult (Goffin, 2000). It can vary from the highly prescriptive and detailed, such as the US intervention programme Direct Instruction System for Teaching and Remediation (DISTAR), through to the more general definition given in the New Zealand, Te Whariki curriculum (New Zealand, 1996), where curriculum is defined as *'the sum total of the experiences, activities and events, whether direct or indirect, which occur within an environment designed to foster children's learning and development'* (p. 10). It is clear that the term curriculum in early childhood can have a much wider meaning than the more traditional view of curriculum as subject-based with prescribed content. This broader definition reflects the complexity and integrated nature of early learning and challenges practitioners to create a curriculum that takes its content from the lives and experiences of the children.

In some cases early childhood 'approaches' quickly become linked to the concept of curriculum. Such is the case with the fluid and emergent curriculum evident in the Reggio Emilia approach (Edwards *et al.* 1995) and also with the more traditional NAEYC document on Developmentally Appropriate Practice (Bredekamp & Copple, 1997). Research suggests that *'flexible curricula, built on inputs from children, teachers and parents, are more suitable in early childhood than detailed, expert-driven curricula'* (OECD, 2002, p. 116).

The New Zealand curriculum has been particularly influential on developing curricular frameworks in the UK and Ireland (NCCA, 2004). Rather than stressing early learning goals and desirable outcomes within defined learning areas, this curriculum, known as the Te Whariki (literally meaning a 'woven mat'), offers guidance in terms of principles and aims. It provides an integrated curriculum across the age range from birth to the age of five and is characterised by a tapestry, or weave, of increasing complexity and

richness. Such an integrated approach also emphasises the importance of considering assessment as pedagogy. The late 1980s heralded
a change in early education in New Zealand. The government
decided to place responsibility for all early educational services
under the auspices of the Ministry of Education. Following a period
of extensive collaboration across the widely diverse cultural groups
within the early education sector, the ministry published what has
become a highly regarded early years curriculum (New Zealand,
1996).

It is difficult to isolate the content of the Te Whariki curriculum,
as it is embedded within the principles and outlined in terms of
learning outcomes associated with each of the identified goals. The
learning outcomes describe various skills, knowledge and attitudes
recommended for children as they develop through the early childhood period. The framework offers guidance on how the outcomes
link in to essential skills and learning areas. Given the holistic
nature of the underpinning philosophy guiding the New Zealand
curriculum, the weave is crafted as a whole rather than being
unravelled into specific aims, objectives and outcomes (New
Zealand, 1996, pp. 93–98). The teacher is challenged to weave
together the various strands of talent and dispositions of the young
child with the agreed areas of learning within a context that reflects
the principles identified as central to a culturally authentic
curriculum. There are four guiding principles in the Te Whariki
document which reflect a re-conceptualisation of what an early
childhood curriculum should include. They are given as empowerment, holistic development, family and community and relationships. They reflect the assimilation of the more contemporary views
of child development emerging from the multitheoretical understanding of the complexity and context-sensitive nature of
development and the interactive nature of learning within and
across contexts. The curriculum is designed to be empowering,
holistic, transactional and ecological (Carr, 1998, p. 2). Such an
approach requires a review of pedagogy and assessment. In

practice, learning and assessment of learning are integrated into the overall pedagogy with teachers documenting development, assessing its meaning and deriving curricular guidance through reflection on their engagement with the children and their evaluation of the considerable and varied documentation maintained, including artwork, photographs, transcribed stories and project materials.

It is in New Zealand that the concept of learning dispositions in early education has most recently been elaborated on and researched (Carr, 1997, 1998, 1999, 2001a, 2001b). Carr has linked the development of certain learning dispositions to the Te Whariki curricular framework. These include: courage (and curiosity) to find something of interest here in the learning community (Curriculum Strand – Belonging); trust that this is a safe place to be involved, focusing one's attention, and encouraging the playfulness that often follows from deep involvement over a period of time (Curriculum Strand – Well-being); perseverance with difficulty or uncertainty (Curriculum Strand – Exploration); confidence to express an idea or a point of view (Curriculum Strand – Communication); and responsibility for justice and fairness and the disposition to take on another point of view (Curriculum Strand – Contribution) (Carr, 1998, p. 4).

To consider the inclusion of dispositions in curriculum goals requires some clarity about what exactly they are. Even those authors advocating attention to dispositions among educators recognise that the concept is messy (Perkins *et al.* 1993) and slippery (Carr, 1998). The concept is considered 'messy' because it invokes a vague assortment of ill-defined or immeasurable behavioural influences – '*dispositions inevitably include reference to things that are genuinely hard to pin down: motivation, affect, sensitivities, values and the like*' (Perkins *et al.*, 1993, p. 18). Carr considers dispositions to be a 'slippery' concept and points out that inclinations must be guessed at from patterns of behaviour exhibited frequently, together with careful observations of the circumstances, observations over time and perhaps discussion with children and their families. The inclination or the intention is not separate from the circumstances, and the unit of analysis of interest becomes the *action* rather than behaviour. Action, therefore, is not simply an observed behaviour but also includes intention and meaning. To understand it requires reflective observations, which move beyond the behaviour to understand the intention (Wertsch, 1991).

The influence of the New Zealand approach can be seen in the emerging Irish Framework for Early Learning. For instance, the framework proposes a thematic approach to learning within the context of four themes: well-being, identity and belonging, communication and exploring and thinking. These interconnected themes are seen as the basis for a holistic curricular approach which places the child at the centre of planning and allows for the creation of learning opportunities which respond to, and are guided by, the child's strengths, interests and needs (NCCA, 2004; 2005).

There has been a great deal written on the subject of early years curriculum in the UK as a consequence of concerns that the national curriculum is impacting negatively on the early years (Cox, 1996; David, 1996a; Drummond, 1996). Many researchers and academics in early education have expressed serious concern that early education, particularly in settings for children of 3–7 years, is being negatively influenced by the downward extension of the primary curriculum with pressure on practitioners to skill children up in preparation for their transition to school (Abbott and Moylett, 1999; David, 1999; Pugh, 1996; Wood, 1999). On the other hand, Rodgers (1999) has been critical of the non-academic approach to early years curriculum development in the UK and criticises the early years lobby, as she characterises them, for relying too heavily on a play-based curriculum with insufficient empirical evidence to support this. Anning (1995) was also critical and, in an effort at guidance, proposed that the basic requirement of a curriculum for 3–7-year-olds must include:

- Positive dispositions to learn
- A firm grasp of the cultural tools and symbols of literacy and numeracy
- Confidence and flexibility in IT
- Practical hand skills and physical capabilities
- Moral understanding and social/emotional skills
- Intellectual curiosity
- Aesthetic and creative abilities.

In the UK, where the compulsory school age is five, there has been an increase in the number of four-year-olds, or 'rising fives', attending the reception classes of primary schools. As a result of concern about the appropriateness of this development, a number of government reports have been published and new policies developed (DFEE, 1997). In a radical departure from the traditional approach, the UK introduced a foundation (pre-compulsory) stage of education. The foundation stage curriculum was developed for those working with children from three years to school age. It was originally organised around early learning goals (QCA, 1999), based on expectations of what most children should be able to do by age five. These were organised around six learning areas that act as the framework for planning a curriculum for four- and five-year-olds. The areas, each providing a series of expressed learning goals and desirable outcomes are:

1. Personal, social and emotional development
2. Communication, language and literacy
3. Mathematical development
4. Knowledge and understanding of the world
5. Physical development, and
6. Creative development.

The documentation highlights the development of personal and social skills, early literacy and numeracy skills, cautioning readers that the areas themselves do not represent a curriculum. There is an enhanced and challenging role for the teacher as the author of the curriculum-in-practice. Although evincing sensitivity to the particular learning style and educational needs of young children, the foundation stage is not without its critics. The design continues in the tradition of a hierarchical and linear format, focusing more on the inputs and outputs of education than on the process. A primary concern expressed is the emphasis it lays on the development of literacy and numeracy skills within the framework of a literacy hour and daily mathematical instruction. Commentators and researchers believe that the positive effects of theoretically sound early education are seriously compromised in practice by simultaneously paying attention to the more traditional emphasis on literacy and numeracy (Pascal & Bertram, 1993; Corsaro, 2003).

The foundation stage framework has been implemented in a wide range of settings serving children under compulsory school age, including nursery schools, private day nurseries, community preschools, accredited childminders and reception classes. It continues to be evaluated, revised and refined (DfES, 2007).

An alternative curricular approach was developed in the UK by the Early Childhood Education Forum and published in their document *Quality in Diversity* (ECEF, 1998). Drawing on the Te Whariki curriculum document from New Zealand, they identify 'foundations for early learning' (pp. 11–12). These are titled:

1. Belonging and connecting
2. Being and becoming
3. Contributing and participating
4. Being active
5. Expressing and thinking; imagining and understanding.

Under each of these foundations, the forum has devised a comprehensive list of goals for early learning. The overall work of the forum focuses on the quality of the early learning experience and presents a dynamic framework from within which to work with all young children under five in the UK.

Most children in the United States commence elementary school at six years of age, although a high proportion of five-year-olds attend non-mandatory kindergarten. Economic comparators indicate that there is limited public funding for early education in the US and the only publicly funded initiatives are interventions funded through the Headstart project. Although some Headstart programmes cater for children from birth to three years, most are designed as interventions for children from three to six years. All other early years services are locally provided and are run as for-profit or not-for-profit services. While there are a wide variety of programmes run throughout the US, the High/Scope programme is one of the best known and evaluated and has been taken by certain states as the state-wide curriculum. High/Scope is both an approach to practice and a curriculum with content based around a series of key developmental indicators (KDIs). The original High/Scope curriculum emerged from one of the earliest intervention programmes known as the Perry Preschool Project. This project forms the basis of an influential longitudinal study, which is still reporting and has found long-lasting social and educational effects sustained over thirty years (Schweinhart & Weikart, 1997). This curriculum is used in certain settings in Ireland. The 'key development indicators' or statements of the High/Scope curriculum describe the social, cognitive and physical development of children from infancy to the age of five. The 'key experiences' are clustered under topic headings which reflect their Piagetian origin: creative representation; language and literacy; initiative and social relations; movement; music; classification; seriation; number; space and time. The task of the adult is to provide an environment in which these key experiences can occur, to recognise and support them and then to build on them with the child.

In the US the document on developmentally appropriate practice (DAP), published by the National Association for the Education of Young Children (Bredekamp, 1987; Bredekamp & Copple, 1997), has had a huge influence on practice and the implementation of curricula. There has been some debate as to whether or not this document should be considered a curriculum. Goffin (2000, 2001) argues that it is not a curriculum but a methodology. While this is certainly true, the document has a very clear theoretical context and raises the issue of the close, interwoven relationship between pedagogy and curriculum in early education. Indeed Roopnarine and Johnson (2000) include DAP as an early educational model or approach and Rodgers (1999) refers to DAP as a curriculum, reflecting the blur that exists in early educational discourse between the content of the curriculum and its implementation. Such a blurring could be advantageous, enriching and challenging for early education and can be seen at its best in the Reggio approach.

The Reggio Emilia municipality of Northern Italy (Edwards *et al.*, 1995) has developed one of the most influential early educational programmes to emerge from Europe. It is a publicly supported programme and has become known as the Reggio approach (Abbott & Nutbrown, 2001). Developed by Loris Malaguzzi (1993), the Reggio approach acts as a proxy for the type of early education provided throughout Northern Italy and, to some extent, throughout Italy as a whole (Corsaro, 2003). Services offer full provision to children under six years of age in specially built settings that are staffed by multidisciplinary teams. Children are grouped in mixed age groups with a key teacher for their entire period in the setting and there is close liaison between the early education and the elementary system, and with parents.

There is no written curriculum for early education in Reggio Emilia. Rather the focus of attention is on projects and activities, which act as the content around which early experiences are designed and extended. In the early years settings of Reggio Emilia where children are educated together from birth to the age of six, they speak of the 'hundred languages of children', meaning all the different ways in which children can communicate and through which they can express themselves (Edwards *et al.*, 1995). Children do not spend time in formal classes developing literacy or numeracy skills; instead the interest and curiosity of the children are used by the teachers as a key to their learning. The processes of exploration, experimentation, discovery, representation, transformation, interpretation, creation and evaluation are foregrounded for attention and expression by the teachers, mostly through the use of project work through the arts. Pedagogical practice in Reggio Emilia is dependent on the social constructions, based on assumptions and experiences of both adults and children. In order for teachers to be able to respond appropriately to the children, they build in opportunities for reflection and rigorously maintain large quantities of documentation that are used as a basis for their reflection; a form of continuing professional development. Teaching decisions are made, not on the basis of a prescribed curriculum but on the basis of evidence and experiences that have been analysed.

The important elements of the Reggio Emilia approach do not form a subject-based curriculum, but make up the content of the relationship. The content is not focused on routine and management, but on the work in hand. Shared activities are considered valuable to both children and adults. The benefits of this approach are the active engagement of children in the learning process and the active engagement of the adult in teaching for learning: they are, to all intents and purposes, the 'proximal processes' (Bronfenbrenner & Morris, 1998) or engines of development that are crucial to the development of generative dispositions in the child. The teacher's role is key as there is no prescribed content; the content is that which emerges from the task which becomes a shared curriculum where the problem is set and then solved. This approach allows for rich developments in skills and knowledge in a dispositional milieu which encourages learning dispositions that meet the values of the community.

There has been a lot of international interest in the Reggio approach and many authors have written extensively about the principles and practice (Abbott & Nutbrown, 2001). Gardner

(1995), in his foreword to *The Hundred Languages of Children*, cautions that one cannot transpose something like the Reggio Emilia approach to another country without adapting it appropriately to that culture. He does, however, recognise the approach as valid and appropriate for young children and notes that Reggio Emilia *'epitomises ... an education that is effective and humane: its students undergo a sustained apprenticeship in humanity, one which may last a lifetime'* (p. xiii).

Katz (1995) picks up on the importance of creating a sense of belonging, of relationships, in young children and points to the rich content that such relationships can have. For relationships to be effective they must be about something, to allow for engagement by the child and the adult and to allow for feedback and for guidance. The relationships described in the various reports from Reggio Emilia are akin to the reciprocal scaffolding proposed by Lambert and Clyde (2000).

Katz suggests six lessons to be learnt from Reggio:

1. Children and teachers together examine topics of mutual interest in depth and detail and using a variety of media and approaches.
2. When children are engaged in this way they attend to their work with great care. The work is a form of documentation of the process of their learning, which they evaluate as well as the adults.
3. Early introduction of observational and representational skills does not deter their creativity.
4. The work in the projects provides rich content for the teacher–child interactions.
5. Many features of adult behaviour convey to the children that all aspects of their work are taken seriously.
6. The driving force behind the principles for the programme is community/family rather than industrial/corporate (pp. 36–37).

One of the most striking and radical features of the Reggio approach is the willingness of the teachers to learn from the children. Claxton (1990) argues that 'good teachers', in the traditional sense, may maximise training procedures that enable pupils to succeed at tests or examinations, but it is teachers whom he calls 'mentors' who equip their pupils to be good learners because these 'good learners' are resourceful, creative, persistent and intelligent in the face of change. Reggio practice is not based on the notion of teaching as applied child development: it demands of teachers a clear understanding of child development, a view of what interests children, what children are doing, what is being offered as their learning environment, materials, interactions and context (Hirst, 2001; Moss, 2001). Practice is not the application of a curriculum within a particular pedagogical formula; it is responsive and fluid and acts as the basis for an emergent curriculum.

In the absence of any national guidance on early years curriculum in Ireland, a number of voluntary membership organisations have identified resources or developed guidelines for curricula (Brennan, 2004). In addition, the curricula associated with different approaches to early education, such as Montessori, and to a lesser extent High/Scope and Steiner, are widely used. However, the National Council for Curriculum and Assessment is currently developing, in consultation with the early childhood sector, a national curriculum, or practice guidelines, for early education in Ireland. The *Framework for Early Learning* is being developed for application in all settings for children from birth through to six years of age. In advance of the publication of the framework, the NCCA have published the results of the consultation and three background papers (NCCA, 2004, 2005; French, 2007; Hayes, 2007; Kernan, 2007). The final framework is due to be published in 2008 and is intended to complement existing curricula and create coherence and connectedness across learning throughout early childhood.

Apart from the forthcoming framework, the infant section of the *Primary School Curriculum* is also addressing the early educational curricular needs of children from four to six years of age. The national curriculum for primary schools in Ireland was revised in the 1990s (Ireland, 1999) and covers all primary education within the age range of four to twelve years. It does note the special nature of early childhood and the length of the school day differs slightly for 'infants' and older children. The introduction to the revised curriculum has a specific section on early childhood education which notes that: '*There is a need for a continuing process whereby the child's experience in the infant classes interacts with the developmental experience of home and family. This highlights the importance of the teacher's dual role as carer and educator*' (Ireland, 1999b, p.30). An explanation of play and its role in the curriculum is dealt with separately in the handbooks for each of the eleven subjects. In certain subject areas specific content and skill strands have been identified. For instance, in the science area four content strands are given. These are living things: energy and forces, materials and environment and care. There are two skill development strands: working scientifically and designing and making. Teachers are encouraged to plan for these strands using children's own ideas and teaching methods appropriate to their age and stage of development. Recognising that not all children start school with the same advantages, the section goes on to call for appropriate special intervention in the preschool years and in the early years of school to enable all children to benefit fully from the learning experience that the curriculum has to offer. The curriculum for infants stresses the uniqueness of the child and the particular needs of individual children at this stage of development.

The Revised Primary Curriculum continues to characterise the curriculum in terms of traditional subjects and has added a number of subjects and learning areas to the existing 1971 curriculum. This expansion of the curriculum, along with other developments within the primary system, has several consequences and has created a situation where the discretion time for teachers to adapt their pedagogical approach has diminished. In particular, it limits the attention that can be given to a more integrated approach to practice addressing the affective and metacognitive dimensions of education and, as Morgan (2002) notes, in attempting to get some coverage of every topic, sufficient attention may not be given to developing the higher-order skills of comprehension, comparison and inference. Pellegrini and Blatchford (2000) caution that escalating pressure on teachers to meet the requirements of increasingly crowded curricula limits the time allocated for meaningful play. For it to be legitimised, meaningful and effective in any social or educational goals, play must be a named element of the curriculum.

Play in early education

There is a broad understanding that young children develop in an integrated way and traditionally, in early education in particular, holistic teaching is seen as a way of meeting the needs of the 'whole' child. Teachers of young children know that they learn about the world and learn to solve problems when they play and that play is their way of experimenting with new ideas and practising skills. Wood (1988) notes that while learning is a direct product of the child's interactions with the environment, the adult in educational settings has a critical role in 'contriving' interactions in response to certain explicit educational goals. Such planning is informed by our understanding of the fact that young children learn through play, observation, asking questions, experimenting, making sense of the world and through suggestions, hints, warnings, conversation, shared practical tasks and reminiscences.

Play is one of the many paths to learning for young children and research into children's play has contributed to our understanding of how this may happen (Bruner, Jolly & Sylva, 1985; Dockett, 1999; Moyles, 1988, 1994). While some researchers have argued that play has not actually been proven as the pre-eminent vehicle for young children's learning (Smith, 1986), it still maintains a high status among practitioners. The evidence of how play impacts on early learning is difficult to identify, but there is overwhelming agreement that play is a powerful medium through which children learn. It is difficult to isolate the causal link between play and learning and it will look different in different cultural contexts (Bruce, 2001). Nonetheless reviews of the importance of play in early education (Bruce, 1997; Moyles, 1994; Pellegrini & Smith, 1998) all point to the value of play in the learning of young children. In addition, Sayeed and Guerin (2000) make a cogent argument for considering the importance of play in early educational interventions for children with additional needs. While ideologically the case for play is strong (Abbott, 1994; Bennett, Wood & Rogers, 1997), some authors argue that the empirical research showing why it is so valuable is limited (David, Aubrey, Anning & Calder, 2003; Rodgers, 1999).

Relationships in play

Play provides multiple opportunities for child-to-child interactions and also opportunities for adults to interact with children and understand their world in order to support their learning and development. The child is influenced by the experience of play, but also influences the environment through play. Adults can facilitate and support play for the child and play with the child but also use play, through reflective observation, to plan for the child and to snapshot the dynamic development of the child. Through reflective observation, adults can extend and enhance the child's play and learning. Sylva *et al.* (1980) evaluated play according to the degree of cognitive challenge and found that cognitive complexity was associated with a greater degree of adult interaction. Careful observation of even very young children indicates that they enjoy playful interactions with peers. These engagements provide a rich space in the curriculum for exploration and play and enhance the overall experience of young children (Singer & de Haan, 2007). Play is common to a wide range of activities and is a valuable source of information on children and a useful basis for assessment. The idea of an interactionist approach to assessment, or assessment as pedagogy (Carr, 2001a), allows for recording children's current level of functioning through reflective observation of dynamic development rather than measuring it against a norm; it acts as a basis for programme planning and/or intervention and as a method for evaluating change and highlighting the impact of the programme or intervention (Moyles, 1988; Sayeed & Guerin, 2000). The interactionist approach emerges from a socio-cultural perspective and emphasises the immediate value of experiences to children rather than focusing on future goals.

As well as the socio-cultural dimension, play has a developmental dimension as proposed by Pellegrini & Bjorklund (1998). In their consideration of continuity in development, they identified heterotypic continuity where a particular behaviour at one age can be clearly linked to a different but related behaviour at a later age. The example given is make-believe play at age three with its emphasis on representing the world with different toys related to reading at a later age where symbols are representative. The point here is that facilitating make-believe play has a legitimacy and appropriateness in terms of literacy that the early introduction of, for instance, pre-reading materials to enhance literacy skills, may not. Similarly, in science teaching, activities can be planned to allow for the use of Hutt's model of epistemic and ludic play (Hutt *et al.*, 1989), where environments are created to allow children explore and ask 'what does this do?' and move from this to the creative, ludic phase of 'what can I do with this?' using the knowledge they have gained through their learning.

Bruce (1991) has argued that play is important in the early years because of its integrating function; that is, through play children find out new information, rearrange old knowledge, integrate and practise in play and, through this process, learn more about their world. She also describes the rhythms of play, their ebb and flow, and notes that *'play is not a static equilibrium or a steady state. It keeps changing according to the time of day, the situation and the people'* (1999, p. 37). This dynamic is also celebrated by Drummond (1999) in her call for a recognition of the real importance of play in children's lives and learning, where she describes how four- to six-year-olds can become engrossed in complex and collaborative play which challenges and strengthens their learning. Gardner (1993) challenges educators and parents to reconsider the values informing the early education and care of children and to reassess the type of childhood we should support if we are to enable the development of different intelligences. This calls for a reconsideration of the knowledge and skills society values, a broadening of our concept of what knowledge is important, what behaviour is intelligent and how to uncover other intelligences previously overlooked (Lyons, 2002). To achieve this *'we need to throw out limiting old assumptions and respect the flexibility, creativity, adventurousness, resourcefulness and generativity of the young mind'* (Gardner, 1993, p.107). Providing the space, time, materials and encouragement for play, as part of the education of young children, is one place to start.

Under the Rules for National Schools, which cover all aspects of school functioning in Ireland, there is limited reference to play, which is clearly separated from the work of the day. Under the section on length of day, the rules define a minimum day as five hours and forty minutes. Within this time it is recommended, but not obligatory, that there be a recreational period of 30 minutes and two five-minute breaks, one in the morning and one in the afternoon. Anything further in the line of play provision must take place in the context of an extended day. Neither of the Acts governing schools – the Education Act 1998 (Ireland, 1998b) and the Education (Welfare) Act 2000 (Ireland, 2000b) – make any direct reference to play. The *White Paper on Early Education*

(1999a) has some limited references to play in education, noting the importance of learning through play for young children (p. 56) but not expanding on the point. The Irish *Primary School Curriculum* (1999b) recommends the use of play in teaching and suggests play as a methodology to be used by teachers in all areas of the curriculum at all levels, but identifies play as most effective at the junior- and senior-infant levels. The emphasis is on the adult use of play as a teaching method rather than engaging with the process of play as education in and of itself.

Research reviewing different approaches to early education indicates the importance of practice that allows children to direct and make decisions about their learning based on, among other things, their own interests and past experiences. The recognition of the powerful role of play as a pathway to learning in this way has been evident in early education literature from the first writings in the field. It is through play that children interact with, explore and extend their environment to gain in their understanding and mastery of it, influencing both their affective and cognitive development. The importance of play in early education is widely acknowledged in Ireland (Brennan, 2004; Carswell, 2002; Hayes, 1995; Ireland, 1999a, 1999b; Kernan, 2006). For instance, the curriculum for the infant classes is *'based on the uniqueness of the child and the particular needs of individual children at this stage of development. The informality of the learning experience inherent in it, and the emphasis it gives to the element of play, are particularly suited to the learning needs of young children'*(Ireland, 1999b, p. 30).

The theoretical endorsement of play and the informality of learning experiences in the early years are not always evident in observed practices with children, particularly within the infant classes at primary school (Hayes *et al.*, 1997; INTO, 1995; Murphy, 2004; OECD, 2004). This finding is not unusual, and concern has been expressed among early educationalists that primary teachers may underestimate the value of play and view it in opposition to the formal education, the 'real work' of the classroom. Where play is used, it is often as a reward for work well done or as a means of introducing elements of more formal education in an 'interesting' way. Glassman and Whaley (2000) use the example of teachers using cars and ramps to introduce children to the concept of gravity or the relationship between mass and speed. This approach to using activity or play to teach according to the prescribed curricular or adult aims is the type of practice that Dewey (1916/1944) considered 'soft', and informed by a 'soup kitchen' theory of education. Glassman and Whaley suggest that this tendency shows a poor understanding of the potential of play as the transparent, immediate activity of the child while work could be considered in terms of the adults' creation of a context to facilitate the child's education. It can be difficult to teach through a play-based curriculum in the face of pressure for formal reading, writing and arithmetic and beliefs that the earlier one starts the better the child will be in literacy and numeracy, in spite of evidence to the contrary. It is not the appropriateness of content that is necessarily problematic, but the appropriateness of the pedagogical approach (David, 1999; Bennett *et al.*, 1996). In addition to the difficulties within the infant classes, however, existing evidence suggests that the use of play in other Irish early years settings may often occur in the absence of any explicit recognition of its developmental potential or within a theorised curricular frame (Hayes, 2007; Kernan, 2007) and thus may be of limited educational value.

Content and implementation of early years curricula

Looking at the early years curriculum from the point of view of the development of the young child raises the question: what should be learned? Schools and, increasingly, preschools are deliberately designed to enhance development and learning and to foster knowledge and skill acquisition. Where there is a specific curriculum described, it generally highlights more traditional areas, such as literacy and numeracy skills. Individual motivation – the inclination, the disposition to learn, is also influenced, one way or another, by early learning experiences, but is rarely explicitly noted among the curriculum goals. While educators recognise that it is possible to have skills but to lack the inclination, wish or habit to use them, the literature on curriculum in Ireland to date gives little or no attention to this aspect of the individual's contribution to development.

The recognition that the fostering of dispositions should be a role of education is not a new idea. It is evident in the works of Dewey (1938/1998) where he presents the notion of fostering 'good habits of mind' and was reintroduced into the education debate by Resnick (1987) before being taken up by Katz (1988) in the early education literature. Apart from their value as a developmental goal for education, dispositions can be seen as an explanatory construct for cognitive behaviour and, in the bio-ecological model of development, Bronfenbrenner and Morris (1998) distinguish between capability and disposition in the developing individual.

Research confirms that learning dispositions are important for development in young children (Sylva, 1994a; 1994b; Katz, 1993; Goleman, 1996; Smiley & Dweck, 1994; Kamin & Dweck, 1999) as they impact on present learning while influencing learning in the future. Sylva (1994b), drawing together the strands of research from various disciplines, concludes that *'preschool experiences put in motion a virtuous cycle of learning orientation at school entry, followed by teacher recognition and expectation, followed by pupil self-concept, school commitment and finally success in adult life'* (p. 162).

In reviewing the goals in early education, Katz (1988) identified dispositions as a separate goal for development, distinct from knowledge, skills and feelings. Carr argues the case for keeping them closely aligned on the basis that the more knowledge and skill one has in a particular topic or activity, the more one is, usually, inclined to become involved in it. This argument is resonant with Dewey's challenge to teachers to reform teaching by attending to the experiences of the learners and building on them to create new knowledge from the old (Dewey, 1916/1944; 1938/1998).

The studies by Dweck and her colleagues over the last two decades into motivation and beliefs in young children suggest that when children consider intelligence as something that develops through their own contribution and effort – *is incremental* – quality learning is the outcome. In addition, she found that teachers are more likely to give positive feedback on effort and children's own contributions if they consider learning to be a balance between an individual's capability and their dispositions. This dual impact has a positive influence on children's sense of themselves as learners, even from a very early age. Learning or mastery-oriented children tend to exhibit positive learning dispositions and maintain persistence in the face of difficulty, locating any difficulty or problem in the context rather than within themselves. Where children consider intelligence as something they either possess or do not possess – *an entity* – then learning is reduced to performance. Children who are performance-oriented seem to assume that their ability to learn and their success on learning tasks is a measure of their own ability alone. Their goal is to achieve a sufficient level of performance for the reward available rather than to persist at a problem so that they might learn how to solve it and proceed.

Traditionally, curriculum and assessment have tended to prioritise capabilities over the motivation or inclination to learn because they are easier to define and measure and much less vague to articulate and assess. Sylva (1994a) poses the question '*how do … adaptive and dysfunctional attributions begin … are they present at the very start of school?*' (p. 92). She refers to evidence from many sources that suggest young children strive for mastery but notes that, by middle childhood, many children have abandoned mastery behaviours because of negative feedback and they opt for performance behaviours instead, a tendency also noted with concern by Donaldson (1978) in her influential book, *Children's Minds*. A key point is that learning-oriented children seem to have an awareness or even an understanding that learning does not depend on any single characteristic, such as ability, but rather on a combination of factors, including the disposition to learn and the degree to which the environment and the people in it support learning over performance. A curriculum which specifically recognises and names dispositions as central to positive development challenges the practitioner to create a learning environment that is likely to yield generative dispositions (Bronfenbrenner & Morris, 1998).

Early childhood experiences have an important role to play in the development of dispositions and attitudes to learning. The adult is central to shaping and guiding dispositional development (Resnick, 1987; Katz, 1993; Carr, 1998, 2001b). Resnick (1987) wrote of the importance of shaping dispositions to assist the development of critical thinking and noted that much of the shaping of the disposition is about learning to recognise and search for opportunities to apply one's abilities. Quality early education, whether in a crèche, a childminder's, a preschool or an infant class, provides such opportunities but is also instrumental in shaping the disposition through careful observation of children in order to identify the emerging dispositions particular to individual children at particular times and in particular contexts. Feedback to children from the learning environment needs to be clear, explicitly articulating the features of the context, the task, the process and their function in it. Research indicates that responsiveness and vulnerability to adult criticism can be seen by the age of five and it has been associated with the same views on the immutability of personal traits found in older children with 'helpless' orientations (Heyman *et al.*, 1992). The work of Dweck and her colleagues, from an individual psychology viewpoint, has shed important light on the influence of the socio-cultural and historical contexts on the development of learner identity, a development with the potential for influencing the quality of present learning and the direction of future learning. Dweck and Leggett (1988) note that 'adaptive individuals' coordinate learning and performance orientations effectively.

While it may be adaptive for children to coordinate learning and performance orientations in certain situations, contemporary education policy in the West emphasises the importance of children learning to learn and developing an identity as a learner early in their education (Katz, 1993; Carr, 1998). Adult sensitivity to the varied goals of education that may compete with this will affect the learning environment. There is concern that current trends in early education may be presenting curricula and environments that encourage a performance rather than a learning orientation and commentators such as Bennett (2005) have specifically cautioned against the 'schoolification' of early childhood settings. Learning environments that encourage a mastery or learning orientation as opposed to a performance orientation in children will be characterised by what Carr (2001) calls an enabling 'dispositional milieu'.

In their review of different early childhood education and care (ECEC) policies, the OECD (2000) note that *'when ECEC focuses primarily on familiarising children with early schooling, there is a risk of downward pressure from a school-based agenda to teach specific skills and knowledge in the early years, especially with regard to literacy and numeracy'* (p. 41). They go on to point out that it seems that *'if countries choose to adopt a view of the child as full of potential and capable of learning from birth, and a view of childhood as an important stage in its own right, then ECEC provision can be concerned with both the present and the future'* (p. 43).

The OECD thematic review reports (2000, 2006) note that several countries identify either subject or learning areas in their curriculum documents. Many of the countries, including the UK and the US, built curricula around defined specific skills which children should master prior to school entry. Denmark and Sweden were untypical and did not identify subject areas or specific skills. They locate their early education curriculum within the wider curriculum framework for elementary and secondary school and describe principles to guide practice across all levels. The OECD report cautions other countries against simply adopting this approach to curriculum design as, without careful consideration, it might lead to a downward pressure from school-based curricula for older age groups, although there is no evidence of this occurring in either Denmark or Sweden. The policy on early education in Norway reflects a particular view of childhood common to most Scandinavian countries. Early childhood is considered a specific phase of life with *'high intrinsic value, and children's own free time, own culture and play are fundamentally important … the need for control and management must at all times be weighed against the children's need to be children on their own premises and based on their own interests'* (Norwegian Ministry of Children and Family Affairs, 1996). This view of childhood recognises the need for children to develop skills and learning appropriate for later schooling while conceptualising children as competent learners, discovering and exploring their immediate surroundings and developing confidence in their own abilities. Endorsing the integrated approach found in Scandinavian countries, where early educational services are based on a belief in democratic values and build on societal values such as community spirit, valuing children, individual freedom and rights, equality and respect for human life and the environment, the OECD suggest that other countries should consider this approach and surmise that primary schools might change and *'develop new ways of understanding children's learning across a wider age span'* (OECD, 2000, p.113).

Curriculum principles in early education

Written curricula generally identify a number of guiding principles that underpin the content and themes presented. The UK Foundation Stage (DfES, 2007), for instance, identifies six principles, each with four commitments describing the principle in practice. They are loosely organised around working in partnership with children and their parents to encourage a sense of belonging for the child in rich learning environments that are well organised by trained staff.

Examples reflecting the principles in practice are explored. Central and local government are responsible for ensuring that services and supports that encourage children's cognitive, social, emotional and physical development and meet parents' need for support for themselves and day care for their children are available for families.

The principles underpinning the New Zealand curriculum are more dynamic and are presented as part of a complex weave of interacting elements, reflecting the weave of cultures and practices found within New Zealand and captured in the title of the curriculum, Te Whariki, a weave. Unlike those in the UK Foundation, the New Zealand principles address the age range from birth to six–five years old and are brief and less specific. They suggest that an early years curriculum should:

(i)   empower children (equip them with the tools to capitalise on and extend their learning);
(ii)   take a holistic approach to learning and development;
(iii)   create systematic links to parents and the community; and
(iv)   encourage and provide responsive relationships.

These principles are then linked to aims addressing four interacting, or woven, strands, each with identified goals. The aims are to facilitate:

(i)   the well–being of the children (nurture and protect);
(ii)   belonging for children and their families;
(iii)   communication through reciprocal relationships at all levels; and
(iv)   exploration that recognises active learning as the means for learning and for constructing meaning.

Drawing explicitly on the work of Piaget and Dewey, and also covering the full age span of early childhood, the following are the principles that guide practitioners in the High/Scope curriculum:

(i)   active learning – through which children construct knowledge that helps them make sense of their world;

(ii)   positive adult–child interactions – central to facilitating active learning;

(iii) a child-friendly learning environment – organised into specific interest areas containing a wide range of well-labelled materials to support children's interests;

(iv)   a consistent daily routine, carefully managed and including the 'plan-do-review' process which enables children to express their intentions, carry them out and reflect on what they have done; and

(v)   team-based daily assessment to allow for individualised curricular planning (Hohman & Weikart, 1995, pp. 5–7).

Within this approach, learning is conceptualised as developmental change and is characterised as a complex physical and mental process. The role of the adult is to support children in their learning through observation and interaction. The 'plan-do-review' method, developed by the High/Scope team and central to their model of practice, was established with the intention of facilitating the development of metacognitive and cognitive skills.

In keeping with the dynamic, integrated and interactionist approach to young children's learning evident in the Reggio Emilia approach, it is not easy to find a list of principles underpinning their 'emergent curriculum'. However, in talking about the way in which the curriculum for early education emerges within the social constructivist tradition of development, Rinaldi (1995) makes the point that the primary principle guiding the work of Reggio Emilia is the image of the child: '*The cornerstone of our experience, based on practice, theory and research, is the image of the children as rich, strong and powerful. The emphasis is placed on seeing the children as unique subjects with rights rather than simply needs. They have potential, plasticity, the desire to grow, curiosity, the ability to be amazed and the desire to relate to other people and to communicate'* (p.102). The team in Reggio settings work together to create an enabling, learning environment to build on the rich potential of each child.

The Irish revised curriculum, which includes the educational frame for four- and five-year-olds, builds on the previous primary curriculum published in 1971 and is guided by seventeen principles, which are an extension and elaboration of the original five principles underpinning the original curriculum. The five principles are:

(i)   the full and harmonious development of the child;
(ii)   the importance of making due allowance for individual difference;
(iii)   the importance of activity and discovery method;
(iv)   the integrated nature of the curriculum; and
(v)   the importance of environment-based learning.

The revised curriculum alters the first two principles to celebrate the uniqueness of the child and to ensure the development of the child's full potential. The remaining three principles, identified as pedagogical principles, are subsumed into a *'wider range of learning principles that help to characterise more fully the learning process that the revised curriculum envisages'* (Ireland, 1999a, p. 9).

In preparing the *Framework for Early Learning*, the NCCA note that the principles informing the process include how best to support children's learning, recognising and respecting their individuality as young learners. The NCCA are using a thematic approach to inform the development of the framework. This involves learning being presented through four themes: well-being, identity and belonging, communication, and exploring and thinking. These themes will be expanded on to promote the holistic nature of early learning, and place the child firmly at the centre of planning for and creating learning opportunities which respond to his/her strengths, interests and needs.

SUMMARY

There are many different models of early education and this section has taken a sample to illustrate the differing contexts in which curricula develop, the content and practices that emerge and the principles that drive such developments. The principles and values guiding curricular frameworks, and influencing both policy and pedagogy, are themselves influenced by social and cultural factors. In various reviews, two distinct groups can be identified: those providing early education to children as a preparation for school and those recognising children as active agents and competent learners where practice is guided as much by children's interests as by adult planning.

The examples presented here were chosen because they illustrate different policy and theoretical approaches to early education. The curriculum models and pedagogy developed in New Zealand and Italy, and those which have been popular for many years in Scandinavia, are presented as being more in harmony with our current understanding of the complexity of early learning and the challenges to pedagogy than the models from the US and the UK. While none of the models is directly transposable to a different culture, they all provide useful frameworks against which to judge the current curricular developments and practices in Ireland.

Points for reflection

It is somewhat daunting to consider the curriculum as *'the sum total of the experiences, activities and events, whether direct or indirect, which occur within an environment designed to foster children's learning and development'* (New Zealand, 1996, p. 10). From your own experiences, directly from your work and drawing on your reading, consider the quality of the curriculum provided for children in Irish early years settings. What principles and values guide the curriculum you are most familiar with, and what does this say about the construction of young children and early childhood in Ireland?

This chapter places the child at the centre of curriculum content and suggests that the adult is the architect of an emerging curriculum. Reflecting on this, explore your own contribution to the curriculum experienced by the children you work with.

Chapter six

A Nurturing Pedagogy in Practice

INTRODUCTION

This chapter introduces the concept of a nurturing pedagogy, a style of practice that integrates care and education to facilitate and transform learning and is explicit in engaging dynamically with children. To set the context it revisits some of the key points raised in previous chapters.

Given the integrated nature of early learning, it is difficult to separate curriculum from practice when writing about early education. However, deriving from the exploration of early years curriculum in the last chapter, this chapter turns attention to practice. It introduces and brings together the terms 'pedagogy' and 'nurture' and elaborates on the idea of a nurturing pedagogy. The use of the term 'nurture' is intended to foreground the educative nature of care and to place as central the critical and active role of the adult in effective, engaging and quality early education.

John Dewey in *Experience and Education* wrote that '*mankind ... is given to formulating its beliefs in terms of Either-Ors, between which it recognises no intermediate possibilities*' (1938/1998, p. 1). This tendency can be particularly problematic when considering dynamic processes such as early education; while it is useful to separate the elements of the process for particular consideration, it is critical to recognise the integrated and integrating reality of the process. The importance of moving away from focusing on the adult, the child or the activity in isolation towards a more integrated and dynamic view of practice, with a focus on interactions as a unit of analysis, has attracted attention among contemporary educational researchers (Sylva, 1997; Wertsch, 1998). Attending to the complexity of interactions, both between children themselves and between children and adults, in early education recognises that the child's own dynamic development within context must be included as an influencing factor in the early educational process itself.

Contemporary research now supports the view that early education curriculum and pedagogy should be broad and holistic, with a greater emphasis on development goals than on subject outcomes (Bredekamp & Copple, 1997; New Zealand, 1996); more process related and co-constructive (Bowman *et al.*, 2001; Lambert & Clyde, 2000); defined by the vital interests and needs of children, families and community (Abbott & Moylett, 1999); and more in tune with socio-cultural contexts (Woodhead, 1999). This supports the development of flexible curricular frameworks that give freedom for adaptation, experimentation and cultural inputs in practice (OECD, 2002. p. 116).

Planning for learning in early education

To capture the integrated and dynamic nature of education, Dewey (1916/1944) wrote of the continuous process of education and the critical role of the adult, emphasising the active role of the child in the process. He stressed the importance of interest as a motivating force for activity and reflection and saw the role of the adult in the process as that of guide or mentor. The classroom environment should be democratic so that children have the opportunity to develop those skills essential to participation in a democracy, a view very much to the fore in early educational discourse today (Moss, 2007). Dewey argued that for effective education, with both short- and long-term impact, curricular aims and content are best derived from the interests and activities of the child. He called on educators to recognise the child as a social individual and encouraged teachers to consider and use children's own experiences and interests as the basis for their practice. Despite acknowledging the individual potential of each child, he was critical of the child study movement which, he argued, overestimated the maturational and biological basis of learning and development (1902/1956). His view of learning as the remaking of the old through union with the new resonates with contemporary attention to the wider context of learning. It captures the idea of construction and reconstruction of knowledge. From this perspective learning is characterised as active, social, dynamic and transforming. The process itself is a key part of the educational experience and one which deserves analysis in and of itself.

In many ways Dewey's views of child development and learning, which were ahead of their time, suffered from the absence of a contemporary psychological framework (Hilgard, 1996). The data emerging from current child development research, as outlined in preceding chapters, support many of Dewey's assertions about how best practitioners can facilitate learning in a way that is meaningful to the child as well as a democratic society. His ideas on educational practice, strengthened by supporting contemporary developmental research, are, once again, informing innovative practices and curricular models within early education (Cuffaro, 1995; Darling & Nisbet, 2000; Glassman & Whaley, 2000; Tanner, 1997). At the time he was writing Dewey was criticised for proposing a 'soft pedagogy' by James (cited in Hilgard, 1996), who dismissed the idea of allowing children to learn through active exploration and examination of materials. Dewey countered by pointing out that it was the misinterpretation of his ideas rather than the ideas themselves that caused difficulty. In respect of interest as a central element in motivating learning, he agreed that where *'interest is taken to mean merely the effect of an object upon personal advantage or disadvantage, success or failure ... [the] procedure is properly stigmatised as "soft" pedagogy; as a "soup-kitchen" theory of education'* (1916/1944. p. 126). For Dewey, interest is far more than this. It emerges from the child and connects things that may be distant. It prompts linkages, through action, problem-solving and the use of materials, which extend children's learning. Further misinterpretations of his ideas within the progressive education movement led to an over-emphasis on the freedom of the child in education, with teachers playing a more distant and unobtrusive role than he would have advocated (Ryan, 1995). However, such extreme interpretations are the exception, with most early education settings offering some blend of child-centred and teacher-directed instruction.

The traditional polarity between teacher-directed and child-initiated early education programmes can be characterised as a difference in focus: a focus on either an academic or an activity/play-based curriculum. As the name suggests, an academic programme is guided by the content of the curriculum and the expected outcomes. On the other hand, an activity or play-based programme functions in the belief that learning occurs as a result of activity. Given our current understanding of the complex nature of learning, neither of these two approaches is sufficient. On the value of child-initiated (activity) over teacher-directed (academic) programmes, Leseman, Rollenberg and Rispens (2001), in a comparison of different models of Dutch early educational provision, argue that within the constraints of the Dutch kindergarten curriculum, free play (child-initiated) was found to be superior from the socio-cultural point of view. In the Irish context it appears, from the limited research available, that for the older preschool age group the academic, teacher-directed approach predominates in primary school classrooms and the activity or play-based approach predominates in preschools (Hayes *et al.*,

1997; Horgan, 1995; Murphy, 2004). Finding a way to balance the two approaches, a way that captures the dynamic, continuous process of education in practice – for both the child and the adult – is a challenge for early education.

Researchers have found the most effective early education practice is that which has a clear theoretical basis (Marcon, 1999). Generally speaking, practice is informed by the values and principles of settings, and early childhood settings can be informed by a variety of different curricula, approaches and models. In Ireland these include the High/Scope approach, the Montessori method and the primary curriculum of the infant classes of the primary school. Emphasising the dynamic nature of early education and the multi-layered effect of the processes on those involved, and on the processes themselves, has led to a move away from drafting curriculum in the more traditional, prescribed manner of primary and secondary school curricula. There are different views on what the purpose of early education should emphasise in terms of the learning and development of young children. In her book, *Planning an Appropriate Curriculum for Under-fives,* Rodgers (1999) focuses on education as equipping children with the skills to learn from experience in their environment through various forms of representation. She argues that while biological endowment gives us the capacity to experience the environment, it is through culture that these capacities are extended. For this reason she argues that it is appropriate for early education practice to focus on the development of representational skills. However, this is not a universally agreed interpretation of children's developmental needs at this age. For instance, Gardner, Torff & Hatch (1996) note that *'until the age of 5 or so – assuming a sufficiently rich environment, the development of competence within symbolic systems occurs without the necessity of much direct instruction or crafted mediation'* (p. 34). An alternative approach to that proposed by Rodgers would be to look to early education as developing and nurturing those less definable skills, such as motivation, organisation, inclination and attitude to learning, which appear to facilitate the later acquisition and application of the literacy and numeracy skills and competencies valued by primary education. In attending to these dispositional aspects of learning, it is important for practitioners to provide a context that is meaningful and relevant to the child as a learner through interactions and relationships aimed at nurturing the affective dimension of learning within a content-rich context. In this way, while in keeping with current understandings about early learning, it may also impact on those 'basic skills' identified by policymakers as so important to later school success.

There is an international trend towards reconsidering curriculum and practice to ensure that it takes account of child development, contextual variables and the dynamic interactions that are the essence of early education. In some countries, such as New Zealand and Scandinavia, this is being addressed by the emergence of national curricular guidelines or frameworks rather than the traditionally more prescribed curricula typical of primary education, to support educators in their practice. In other countries, for instance the United States, there is no national curriculum, but professional bodies, such as the National Association for the Education of Young Children (NAEYC), have developed national guidelines for practice (Bredekamp, 1987; Bredekamp & Copple, 1997). This trend is causing a move away from formal, didactic modes of instruction and a loosening up of centrally determined curriculum content. The result is greater attention to a pedagogical style that is child and context sensitive, emphasising the social, experiential and active nature of learning (Banks, 2000; David, 1993; Pascal & Bertram, 1993). This move to understand and explain the dynamics of the early learning and teaching processes presents a difficulty in separating pedagogy from curriculum content. They are both central elements of a continuous process, where one depends on the other. This process is less content-bound in early education than in later stages of education, although to be effective in terms of development and learning the practice must be content rich.

Academic curricula are content focused and are generally accompanied by defined and explicit learning goals or desirable outcomes for the child. Goals and objectives are destinations to be reached by the child and, in this way, they tend to be future focused, which limits the attention to the present reality of the process. This orientation has been criticised as being inappropriate for young children, with too much emphasis on the future and insufficient attention on the importance of day-to-day experiences or natural curriculum (Siraj-Blatchford, 2003) on their actual development. Activity-based curricula, on the other hand, attend more to the child's way of learning and emphasise principles rather than goals. This focus on principles and aims allows for greater flexibility and responsiveness to the immediate learning context for the child. However, they too have been criticised, mainly for giving too much attention to the child and relegating the teacher to the position of mere observer.

One of the major problems resulting from the ongoing arguments over curriculum types, goals and methods is that both sides in the struggle may overlook curriculum and teaching methods beyond the traditional either-or dichotomy. The results of many studies suggest that both sides underemphasise and undervalue a third option – namely, curriculum and pedagogy – that addresses children's current interest and the progress of their intellectual development, as distinct from the direct instruction emphasis on academic learning and future outcomes, or the child-initiated learning emphasis on children's play and self-initiated learning in the immediate present (Banks, 2000). This third approach can be called the process approach and its essence is that the curriculum is located within a firm set of principles rather than guided by a set of short-term objectives or goals. These principles allow early education to meet the immediate learning interests of the child and also allow the teacher to plan for future development and learning in line with the individual child's own interest, experience and developmental level.

Learning in action

To understand more about the influence of early education on the development of young children, account should be taken of the contexts in which learning occurs and its meaning for the child and the adult. Increasingly, researchers are undertaking the examination of development within natural contexts. Questions about how young children learn and, in response, how they should be taught, are guiding curricular development and practice, rather than questions about what children should learn and the content of the curriculum. Educators, policymakers and researchers are increasingly seeking to understand what young children do and how they learn rather than merely prescribe what young children should be taught.

We now have evidence that the dynamic approach to early education, which attends to the process over the product, offers more for children's positive development than either the academic or play-based approach alone. Research consistently shows that successful early education facilitates the child in active learning in learning environments or 'dispositional milieu' (Carr, 2001a) that are well planned, where staff are well trained, confident and supported in their work (Ireland, 2002). Interpretation has become central to both children and adults as they participate in the process of early education: children interpreting and making sense of the world, and adults observing, reflecting on and interpreting children's behaviour to plan the curriculum and assessment and guide their practice. From the pedagogical perspective, quality models of early education are characterised by underpinning principles which present a view of the child as an active partner in the integrated and ongoing process of learning, reflecting a strong commitment to developing the social and affective dimensions of learning, as well as the more traditional emphasis on cognitive development. This reflects the views expressed by many, including Rutter (1985), Ball (1994), Sylva (1994a), Bruner (1996) and Carr (2001b), that the most important learning in early education has to do with the 'soft', affective and difficult-to-measure aspects of development, such as aspirations, social skills, motivation, organisation, learner identity and confidence.

As noted earlier, there is a need to consider the balance between attention to the affective and cognitive in early education. Current research suggests a need to emphasise the affective dimension over the traditional, cognitive elements of learning. This does not mean that early education should ignore skills development or knowledge acquisition. Practice aimed at encouraging the development of learning dispositions and metacognitive skills cannot be content-free; indeed it is essential that children's interactions with their environments are challenging and rich in both language and content. This can happen either directly, in terms of the content of social interactions with an adult or advanced peer, or indirectly through the carefully considered provision of materials, objects, activities and opportunities.

There is a crucial role for practitioners to play in enhancing the opportunities for all young children to learn effectively during the early years. There are also implications for early educational curriculum development and pedagogy. There is no point in nurturing affective development and metacognitive skills in a content vacuum. Wood (1988) argues that teaching *'invites interaction, negotiation and the shared construction of experiences'* (p. 210) which enables the child to learn the 'language' of, for instance, mathematics. What does this mean for particular subject areas? In this regard he writes that *'a sound psychology of mathematics would subsume a theory of the (common) conceptions that children bring to bear on mathematics problems. It would also offer a sense of direction as to how, where and when we respond to these. However ... such knowledge would not provide a map of the learner's terrain, though it would improve our sense of direction'* (p. 210). Interactions that are meaningful to the child within a curriculum framework that is relevant to both the teacher and the child are likely to be most effective in terms of positive development and learning.

The evidence suggests that early education that emphasises the affective dimensions of learning and those cognitive skills associated with the planning and organisation of knowledge positively influences children's later academic cognitive development in terms of content knowledge and literacy and numeracy skills. This approach yields foundational short-term benefits and sustainable long-term benefits across social and educational dimensions.

Towards effective learning

Play has an important role in early educational practice, but the language of play can be confusing and contradictory and there are different views about what exactly play means, particularly in the context of education. Is it free choice or is it experiential activities structured by an adult? There are several different definitions of play, reflecting contrasting approaches to its study, and it has been suggested that definitions of play can be usefully considered as either process-led or product-led. Process-led definitions of play attend to aspects of play such as its role in fostering intrinsic motivation, enjoyment, learning, happiness and interactions in context. Product-led approaches, on the other hand, attend to its role in the development of thinking, motor activity, behaviour and preparation for the future.

The overdefinition and overuse of the term 'play' has diminished understanding of its powerful educative value. It has trivialised it to the extent that play has, in certain contexts, come to mean everything and nothing and its value as an integral part of the early education curriculum is weakened. In fact, play can have a dual role in early education. It can provide opportunities for children to explore and learn at their own pace and it can be a very powerful pedagogical tool for the teacher who, through observing play, can plan future opportunities for learning (Hayes, 2003). Through play in a nurturing environment, children develop a model for interpreting the world and their experiences in it. They learn how to negotiate the rules and requirements of their immediate world and make sense of that world. They learn how to learn. It is learning to make sense of the world that dominates early childhood education and characterises it as different from other levels of education. Adults have an important role in creating an environment for the children to facilitate this process.

Hutt *et al.* (1989), in their study of play and learning, proposed that play be considered as having two elements: exploration and play (see chapter 5, p.107 also). This view of play as exploration and learning reflects Dewey's position on the role of play in education. Building on the recognition of the child as an explorer, the teacher can attend to the opportunities that will arise to guide the child's understanding of problems and their solutions. This presents opportunities for the child to construct or co-construct knowledge in activity rather than simply receive information from instruction. Progressive early childhood ideals for learning through play, contemporary emphasis on life-long learning and the role of early education in cultural transmission have all influenced the study of play in early education. But there is another element of the study of play that is attracting attention: playfulness. Attention to the idea of playfulness is not new; Dewey (1902/1956) noted that playfulness, rather than play itself, was important to children's learning. In research on learning dispositions in early education, playfulness has been identified as one of the dispositions to be fostered (Carr, 2001b, 2002; Claxton, 1999). Playfulness ensures that play is a self-motivating and enjoyable process that leads to learning. It encourages experimentation, de-emphasises the need to be perfect, and it builds self-esteem. Playful children are curious, ask questions, take time to explore, try to understand, use prediction to form, test and evaluate ideas. However, the tendency to 'schoolification' within early education (Bennett, 2006) and pressures of primary-like curricula act as barriers to the development of playful learners (Parker-Rees, 1999).

Shifting attention from *what* we should teach young children in early education to questioning *how* best to achieve 'effective learning' through 'effective teaching' creates new challenges for practice. There is sufficient understanding of development and learning to describe what 'effective learning' might look like in practice. In their description of 'intelligence-in-practice', Resnick & Nelson-Le Gall (1997) capture some of the features of effective learning. Children who are considered 'intelligent-in-practice' believe that they have the right (and the obligation) to understand and make things work; that problems can be analysed, that solutions often come from such analysis and that they are capable of that analysis. They have a variety of problem-solving skills and good intuitions about when to use them; know how to ask questions, seek help and get enough information to solve problems and have habits of mind, or dispositions, that lead them to actively use these various skills and strategies for acquiring information (pp. 149–150). Central to this development is the learner's identity of self as a learner and a sense of belonging to the learning community (Carr, 1998; Pascal & Bertram, 1993; Sylva, 1994a). This attention to the active participation of the child resonates with parallel developments with respect to children's rights and children's visibility in the learning process in general. It challenges educators and policymakers to consider what it means to facilitate such active participation, particularly in early education; it further challenges us to consider what knowledge we should attend to in early education.

Development of affective, cognitive and metacognitive skills commences in the earliest years of life. Differences in motivational and belief systems in learners, and associated institutional support systems, can be detected in young children during early education (Dweck, 1999; Katz & Chard, 1994; Tobin, Wu and Davidson, 1989). Modern pedagogy is moving increasingly towards the view that educators should equip children with a good understanding of how they think and how they organise knowledge and information rather than simply giving them the knowledge or information. Bruner (1996) contends that *'the child should be aware of her thought processes, and that it is crucial for the pedagogical theorist and teacher alike to help her to become more metacognitive – to be as aware of how she goes about her learning and thinking as she is about the subject matter she is studying. Achieving skill and accumulating knowledge are not enough'* (p. 64). The affective and cognitive abilities described can be developed through attending to the quality of interactions, communication and relations between individuals and their social environment. This, in turn, can reinforce the development of a sense of belonging, connectedness and community identity – critical foundations for later educational and social success.

Fostering the development of both the metacognitive and affective dimension to learning in early education can enable children to become ready, willing and able learners (Carr, 2001b). Such development and learning is particularly important in young children as it facilitates the acquisition, comprehension, retention and application of what is learned, assists learning efficiency, critical thinking and problem-solving, and gives children control or self-regulation over thinking and learning processes and products.

Developing a nurturing pedagogy

The degree to which a state involves itself in early education and the extent to which early education is regarded as a care/welfare or an educational aspect of policy influences the funding, focus and the status of early education and, in turn, the process of early education itself. From the thematic review of early childhood education and care policy across twelve countries carried out by the OECD (2000 and 2006), it is evident that reasons for investing in early education are embedded in cultural and societal beliefs about young children, the role of the family and of government and the purpose of early education. Different systems are driven by different beliefs, and values about early childhood and early educational practices vary accordingly. Variations reflect the different values and understandings societies have concerning how and what young children learn. These values and beliefs inform the design of curricula, the location and support of services, the role of the adult and the degree of involvement of children in the process. The decision on where to provide early education and what that education might look like are policy decisions, which influence the learning experiences of young children.

In the context of the continuing distinction made between care and education in certain countries, including Ireland, a distinction which mirrors that made between play-based and academic models of early education, Caldwell (1989) attempted to find a balance by coining the term 'educare'. This concept was intended to bring together care and education as equally important for curriculum development and pedagogy and was meant to describe an approach to education that offered '*a developmentally appropriate mixture of education and care; of stimulation and nurture; of work and play*' (p. 266). Although the term has not really been taken up in the everyday language of early education, it did force further debate about how best to consider these two interconnected elements of early education and, in particular, how to reconceptualise 'care' so that it ranks equally with education in early educational process and practice (Hayes, 2003). One of the obstacles to this is the strong association between the concept of care and that of mothering. To move beyond this, it is necessary to improve our understanding of what it is to be a caring teacher and to acknowledge that it goes far beyond the notion of 'gentle smiles and warm hugs' which obscures the critical developmental and educational value of early education and the complex intellectual challenge of working with young children (Dalli, 2003).

In reading the authors writing in the late nineteenth and early twentieth century, one finds references to nurture rather than care when writing about the needs of younger children. The word 'nurture' has a different tone to it than the word 'care'. In comparing the meaning of the two words, 'nurture' is more engaging and active than 'care'. To care is almost custodial in tone and requires a minimum of interaction; the adult merely provides for and looks after the child. To nurture, on the other hand, conveys a more engaged level of interaction and requires the adult to actively nourish, rear, foster, train and educate the child. Nurturing practitioners facilitate the development of metacognitive awareness and management of cognitive processes. In essence, they assist children in learning how to learn, in recognising themselves as competent and masterful learners who can explore and problem-solve and are sufficiently self-aware to seek assistance when necessary. The language and content context for such practice is guided by the experiences and interests of the children augmented by the practitioner's ability to extend such experience and interest. Such an approach recognises the educative role of care as nurture and both challenges and permits practitioners to give time to planning for the 'soft' and messy aspects of early learning and to encourage playful interaction, exploration, dialogue and collaborative learning to encourage and support young children's learning and to practice a nurturing pedagogy. The learning environment, and children's interaction with it, should be challenging and rich in both language and content.

The title Froebel finally gave to his centres for the education of young children – kindergarten – was intended to capture his belief that young children's learning needed to be nurtured. For this reason he also argued that only women should teach very young children. In his educational facilities, Robert Owen also recognised the importance of play in a nurturing environment when he dictated that children under six years should not be annoyed by books, but should be allowed to play and make music (Tizard & Hughes, 1984). The word nurture – as opposed to care – was used by McMillan (1920) when she claimed that a lack of education and nurture in the first years of life would 'cloud and weaken' all the rest of life (Curtis, 1997).

The caring or nurturing responsibility of the adult, where care is recognised as more than mere 'minding', gives an enhanced educational role to it. Considering care as nurture gives it an active connotation with a responsibility on the adult to provide nurturance and foster learning rather than to simply mind or protect the child. Such a shift in emphasis raises the expectations of how teachers plan and interact in early educational practice. The role of the adult in early childhood education is crucial and multi-faceted (Athey, 1990). It is a combination of listener, questioner, advisor, demonstrator, actor, sympathiser, negotiator, assessor and guide. In addition, the adult must also recognise their role as a 'learner', a reflective observer of children who learns from obser-vation and uses this as the basis for pedagogical practice.

It has been argued that reconceptualising care as nurture would strengthen the attention to the educative value of care and allow for a more appropriate 'nurturing pedagogy' to emerge in early edu-cation learning environments (Hayes, 2003, 2007). If adults are to nurture children's learning they must develop skills of observation and reflection to allow for the non-intrusive planning and provision of a learning environment that supports and extends children's own learning. This allows for increased attention to positive interactions between child and adult and also allows for planning by the adult for future opportunities that might extend the child's own learn-ing; it gives a role to the adult which places the child at the centre. It encourages the movement away from the organisational/managerial role of the teacher – evident from the research into Irish pedagogical practice with young children – and fosters the processes of interaction, dialogue and planning, leading to the shared meaning-making and construction of knowledge.

A nurturing pedagogy (Hayes, 2007) fosters the processes of interaction, dialogue and planning, leading to the shared construc-tion of knowledge. Where the adult is observing and listening to young children and reflecting on these observations, the daily curriculum plan is based on engagement with children, assessment of their interests and developmental levels as well as their needs and the aims of education. Through a reflective and nurturing pedagogy, adults can also identify difficulties in individual development and move to address them, either in the context of the classroom setting or through outside interventions and supports. Implicit in the concept of a nurturing pedagogy is the idea that pedagogy is an integrating process, a guide to an emergent and responsive curriculum (Abbott & Nutbrown, 2001; Edwards *et al.*, 1995) and a medium for assessment (Carr, 2001a; Rogoff, 1997). Finally, a nurturing pedagogy extends the under-lying idea of respect for the child as a participating partner in the learning process while at the same time recognising and articulating a mechanism for respecting the dual nature of early education as care and education.

Professional development for early childhood care and education

It follows that the role of the adult in early education is central to the effectiveness of this pedagogy. Analysis of the various tasks required uncovers a group of functions that fall into management and educational roles, which are intricately interconnected in practice. The management role encompasses planning for children's learning; resourcing and organising opportunities for learning; recording and documenting children's learning; evaluating practice and adapting to the interests and needs of children. The educational role involves reflective observation to inform practice; supporting and extending learning in groups and with individual children; understanding what is happening as children learn; and responding to this understanding and working in partnership with other adults and children themselves in the process that is early education.

The importance of well-educated practitioners is highlighted in the research into effective, quality early childhood care and education (Edwards *et al.*, 1995; Pianta, Howes, Burchinal, Bryant, Clifford, Early and Barbarin, 2005; Weiss, 2005). Bowman and her colleagues (2001) expand on the importance of the adult in early education, particularly identifying those characteristics to be developed through training. Well-trained practitioners are confident in their knowledge of the sophisticated nuances of child development, recognise and respond to the normative and dynamic dimensions of development, and are familiar with the skills and knowledge appropriate to the age group in their setting; they are careful and sympathetic listeners and respectful to children; they negotiate meaning rather than impose it; and they are reflective observers who are able to respond to children and provide sensitive feedback (Abbott & Moylett, 1999; Carr, 2001a; David, 1999; Katz, 1996; Nutbrown, 1996). Such practices are the manifestation of a nurturing pedagogy and embody a trust in the educative value of care in early education.

Johnson (1988) believes that all practitioners come to their practice with informal theories about children's learning and development, informed by their training and their experiences. They derive these theories from experience and often accept them much more readily than they accept the implications of theory and research from so-called child development experts. These implicit beliefs that practitioners have about child development and how children learn are termed 'folk pedagogy' by Bruner (1996) and need to be challenged in the context of contemporary understandings. Professional education and training for early education practitioners require a strong element of child development along with subject knowledge and principles of practice. The potential of the concept of a nurturing pedagogy as an integrating mechanism for care and education, and as a challenge to mainstream training for those working with children in education and care contexts, has been considered in respect of early education by Hayes (2004) and, more generally, by Petrie (2004). Petrie makes the case for using the term pedagogy to reflect the complex roles of those working directly with children and she argues that the term creates the image of a professional space where care and education meet, integrate and become one. She notes the potential of this in practice where the concept of *'pedagogy could foster a unifying ethos across settings and age groups, with many workers in the children's sector reconstructed as pedagogues, sharing common values and approaches* (Petrie, 2004, p. 295). Combining the word pedagogy with the term nurture is intended to strengthen the space where care and education integrate while conveying the notion of an engaged level of interaction, thus providing a rich and theoretically sound context for reforming teaching practice in early education.

If we are to move towards a real acknowledgement of the critical value of both care and education in all early years settings, we will also have to contend with the implications this will have for the professionalisation of the sector. It has been argued that a well-educated workforce working directly with children, sensitive to the complexity of the role, will enhance the quality of early learning experiences for children and ultimately benefit us all (Petrie, 2004; Cameron, 2004). Continuity of experience for children within and across settings, through a shared understanding of practice among practitioners, can contribute to limiting any negative impact of transitions across different settings and facilitate and enhance learning.

The opportunities presented by a shift of focus from the traditional care and education dichotomy to a consideration of the integrated, and integrating, process of early childhood care and education are extensive and challenging. They require a significant change in understanding early education at a policy and practice level and a reform in the education of all those working with children in early years settings. These opportunities and challenges provide a rich environment in which to develop an early childhood care and education system that reflects contemporary Ireland and draws on international research, within our unique cultural context, to the benefit of all our children.

There is no doubt that a move towards more informal practice will require a significant shift in approach away from the more traditional, didactic style of teaching. Dewey (1938/1998) and others

(Bruner, 1996; Carr, 2001a; David, 1999) have noted that the more informal the pedagogy the greater the need for careful structuring of the learning environment. This structure is not reflected in a particularly ordered routine or environment. Rather it is expressed in practice through carefully informed and reflective planning from a rich knowledge base. To effect such a change in practice will require a significant review of and investment in pre-service and in-career education for all those working with young children, whatever the setting (Coolahan, 2002; Dunphy, 2000; Ireland, 2002; Hayes, 2007). The challenges should not be under-estimated. The care and education dichotomy has led to a situation where the care element in early childhood care and education is regarded as the childcare dimension. The dichotomy allows care to be characterised within a child development framework, which de-emphasises the educational nature of the work. This privileges education over care and can be seen in aspects of education supports, pay, conditions of service and influence (McFarlane & Lewis, 2004).

Reconceptualising pedagogy in early education

Recognising the child's part in the process of learning, compatible with the rise in attention from psychological, sociological and rights research (Hayes, 2001; David, 1999), requires a shift in pedagogical approach from the traditional didactic approach of the classroom and the more *laissez-faire* approach of activity-based settings towards what Bruner calls a 'pedagogy of mutuality' (1996, p. 56). Such a pedagogy presumes that all minds are capable of holding ideas and beliefs which, through discussion and interaction, can be moved towards some shared frame of reference. '*It is not simply that this mutualist view is "child-centred", but it is much less patro-nising towards the child's mind. It attempts to build on exchange of understanding between the teacher and the child: to find in the intuitions of the child the roots of systematic knowledge, as Dewey urged*' (p.57). The importance of shaping and nurturing such learning dispositions to assist the development of critical thinking is now becoming a central issue of debate (Carr, 1998, 2001a; Katz, 1995; Resnick & Nelson-LeGall, 1997). The development of generative learning dispositions is largely about learning to recognise and search for opportunities to apply one's abilities. Quality early education environments provide such opportunities and the adult has a key role in shaping disposition through careful observation of children to identify and respond to the emerging dispositions particular to individual children at particular times and in particular contexts. Feedback to children from the learning environment needs to be clear and to articulate explicitly the features of the context, the task, the process and the child's function in it. Fostering the development of both the metacognitive and affective dimension to learning in early education can enable children to become ready, willing and able learners (Carr, 2001b).

For practitioners to assist this process they must consider how best to facilitate the development of metacognitive awareness and management of cognitive processes. They must, in essence, assist children in learning how to learn, in recognising themselves as competent and masterful learners who can explore and problem-solve, are self-aware and seek assistance when necessary. The context for such teaching is guided by the experiences and interests of the children and augmented by the adult's ability to extend such experience and interest.

Adults who practice in this way provide content-rich and risk-rich environments that excite and stimulate the child, but which, at the same time, are secure and safe. The practitioner does not have all the answers; rather, they help the child to find their own answers and resolutions to problems as they arise. Where early education has too strong a knowledge or content focus, emphasising the need for children to know facts before they can apply their learning effectively, practitioners may become uncertain in their role and believe that they have to be the fount of all knowledge. Katz (1996) notes that, in her experience, it is this belief that makes student teachers very anxious, and can lead them to focus their efforts at preparation and planning rather than thinking about appropriate teaching and learning strategies. Recognising the centrality of pedagogy, as well as curricula, to effective early education, is a challenge and requires extensive knowledge accompanied by a trust in the ability and interest of children to learn. In order not to become 'paralysed by uncertainty', teachers of young children must be able to teach with optimum confidence in the rightness of their actions based on robust evidence of child development (Katz, 1996, p.145). However, she continues that they should also be imbued with a healthy scepticism and an ability to question their own practice.

The predominant discourse in ECEC views children as active participants in their own learning where the importance of a sense of belonging and connectedness to their world is emphasised, and where children and adults co-exist in interdependent relations (Dahlberg, Moss & Pence, 1999; Moss and Petrie, 2002). This marks an important shift in the understanding of the role of the adult from passive carer, or reproducer of knowledge, to one where the adult shares in the construction of knowledge and where adults' and children's ongoing, interdependent learning and playfulness in daily practice are important. What might this look like in everyday pedagogical play with babies, toddlers and young children? Drawing on the three overlapping age-related phases of early childhood identified in the NCCA's Framework for Early Learning – babies (birth to 18 months); toddlers (12 months to 3 years); young children (2.5 to 6 years) – this section keeps to the fore the four complementary themes that provide a framework for NCCA's conceptualisation of early learning: well-being; identity and belonging; communicating; exploring and thinking. Rather than attempting to provide an overview of all possible practice approaches in each phase of childhood, the following section raises issues for consideration within the context of selected content and processes to illustrate the relational aspects of play and learning through the lens of the playful, learning child connected to and interdependent with significant adults in their lives (Kernan, 2007).

In the early years of life there is a tension between what is old and what is new, or between the secure, familiar and safe and adventuring outwards to what is novel or represents freedom, facilitating growth and development and a sense of connectedness and belonging to the world (Nabhan & Trimble, 1994; Tuan, 1977). Both are required if babies and toddlers are to thrive. It is helpful when planning for babies and toddlers to draw on a formulation of the play of babies and toddlers utilised by Manning-Morton & Thorp (2003). They identify three groups of fundamental questions, which capture babies' and toddlers' motivation to make sense of the world. The first of these relates to the 'Sense of I': who am I? How does my body work? Who might I be? The second group of questions captures the sense of reaching out and interacting with the other: who are you? How are we the same and different? What can we do together? The third group invokes babies' and toddlers' instinctive curiosity and drive to explore their surrounding physical world: what is it? What does it do? What can I do with it?

In providing a 'secure base' that challenges and protects very young children, it is critical that adults understand the drive to play. This requires adults to 'read' the body language of a baby communicating his/her desire to play or explore or perhaps communicating his/her need to feel secure. Play episodes occur throughout the day, may be embedded in routine care-giving, and are often unplanned. A desire to play may be indicated *by looking out and pointing, crawling away, climbing, running, jumping, hiding,* whilst a need for security may be indicated by *searching, reaching up, hugging, clinging, approaching, following* (Manning-Morton & Thorp, 2003). 'Tuning in to' babies' and toddlers' perceptions of their world is also about adults engaging or appreciating the 'newness' of childhood experience of the environment (Ward, 1978) and maintaining the capacity for sensory experience that may be dulled for adults by familiarity (Tuan, 1974).

By the end of the first year, a great deal of play relates to developing physical and locomotion skills, for which babies exhibit great enthusiasm. When they have the opportunities to explore, risk and try again in an environment that is both safe and challenging, babies can engage in motor practice play that leads to advanced physical abilities, mobility, agility, dexterity and, as a result, confidence, independence and learning. Often their growing competence in walking, running and jumping provides the focus for playful activity (Lindon, 2001).

As the developing and growing child changes in action capabilities over time, so too will the possibilities for action with respect to the environment (Tudge *et al.* 1997). Crawling children and toddlers are challenged by variations in terrain, so the floorscape and small changes of levels in steps and curves are of great interest to these newly mobile children. The importance of experience on diverse ground surfaces, slopes and steps, structures for climbing on, over and under, accessible materials, low windows and direct access between the indoors and outdoors have been outlined in a range of documents describing good design and pedagogical practice indoors and outdoors for babies and toddlers (Bergen, Reid & Torelli, 2001; Manning–Morton & Thorp, 2003; High/ Scope Educational Foundation, 2003). In designing room layouts, it is important to consider pathways and boundaries so that the play environment should provide challenge along with the freedom to move and explore.

With increasing age and language abilities, toddlers and young children are more likely to engage in social play with peers. Pretend play, or fantasy play, emerges in the second year of life, and it is generally considered to peak between three and five years (Rubin, Fein & Vandenberg, 1983). It has been characterised as being part of a package of symbolic abilities, which includes self-awareness, theory of mind and language (Smith, 2006). Unlike other forms of play, it is generally regarded as being uniquely human. It is important for practitioners not to underestimate the importance of such play in terms of social connectivity, children's friendships and their ability to make and maintain friendships over a period to time. Much research has demonstrated the centrality of peer relationships and friendships for young children (Dunn, 1993; Paley, 1992). Research has also highlighted the importance of peer play and socio-dramatic play as a key means of supporting the socio-cognitive processes involved in social well-being and adjustment (Dunn, 1993). Interviews with four- and five-year-old children regarding their experience in early childhood settings in Dublin suggest that the need for affiliation with their (same-sex) peers was hugely important to them (Kernan, 2006).

For many children the early childhood setting is the first exposure to a public arena (Dunn, 1993). Children attending crèches or day nurseries typically spend longer hours daily in the same setting than would be the case in a preschool playgroup or a junior infant classroom. It is important, therefore, that practitioners respect their right to be alone or in very small groups. In seeking places to be apart, young children may be dealing with felt crowdedness in a group setting (Greenman, 2005; Olds, 1988). Small spaces, or 'hidey holes' have been conceptualised as being nest-like, offering comfort, seclusion or time out (Nabhan & Trimble, 1994), meeting the need 'to see without being seen' (Kirkby, 1989), where children can choose play partners and themes in the private spaces of childhood (Brown & Freeman, 2001). (The above section is taken from Kernan, 2007).

The examples of practice outlined above are illustrative of a nurturing pedagogy where the adult engages with the child, drawing on the child's interests and experience. Two practice documents that have the potential to support this pedagogical approach in Ireland are the *Síolta – The National Quality Framework* (CECDE, 2006), and *The Framework for Early Learning* (NCCA, forthcoming). Both these documents are derived from extensive consultation with practitioners and are informed by current research. They locate themselves in a shared understanding of the diversity of early education in Ireland and, although they come from different perspectives, they both present clear principles that underpin the material developed.

Early childhood education is a dynamic enterprise and as groups and group dynamics change, so does practice, and this is part of its reward. Theories of practice change over time: '*No matter how well thought out an approach or instructional plan may be, or how well it seems based on theory, teachers must constantly test their theory-based ideas in the real world. Teachers in this sense are as much researchers as anyone else. Together with other early education professionals, they are or should be active participants in "experimental pedagogy"* ' (Johnson, 1988, pp.17–18). Just as surely as children learn from them, adults learn from the children they work with, and it is reflection upon that knowledge that allows practitioners to respond effectively to individual children.

SUMMARY

This chapter argues that the practitioner in early education has a unique and key role in facilitating and transforming learning and creating rich learning environments for children. Through responding effectively to the complexity of interactions, both between children themselves and between children and adults, in early education, the adult allows space for the child's own dynamic development to contribute to the learning environment. The available evidence suggests that early education practice that is interactive and which emphasises the affective dimensions of learning is most appropriate for positively enhancing children's development in the immediate present and for later academic cognitive development. The idea of a nurturing pedagogy, and the use of the term 'nurture', is intended to foreground the critical and educative nature of care and to place as central the critical and active role of the adult in effective, engaging and quality early education.

Points for reflection

The role of the adult in early educational settings is central to the quality of the early learning experiences of children. In this chapter the concept of a nurturing pedagogy has been explored. Such an approach to practice challenges practitioners to be reflective, active and integrating. Reviewing your own practice, examine the extent to which you learn from the children you work with: is your planning and provision for them challenging? Are you maximising the learning opportunities and engaging with children in the construction of knowledge and meaning-making? Take time to observe your practice as well as the behaviour of the children and the practices of your colleagues. Use carefully recorded observations as the material for discussion and learning on an ongoing basis.

Chapter seven

Creating Inclusive Learning Environments

INTRODUCTION

A central theme of this book is the dynamic and interactive nature of learning. Chapters 4 to 6 highlight the importance of inter-actions between children and between children and adults within the context of 'content- and risk-rich' environments, whereby young children are engaged in interpreting and making sense of the world with the support of observant and responsive adults. A key contributing factor in this process is the design, organisation and resourcing of the physical environments where learning takes place. In this chapter the interactive nature of learning is discussed with particular reference to children's interactions with the physical environments where they spend their time. The National Council for Curriculum and Assessment (NCCA) in *Towards a Framework for Early Learning* (NCCA, 2004) have highlighted the following issues when considering the learning environment:

Firstly, *Outdoor and indoor learning environments should be motivating and inviting to all children, so that they are encouraged and helped to explore and to use all the possibilities offered for fun, adventure, challenge and creativity.* Secondly, *the learning environment needs to support each child's developing sense of self-worth, as well as nurturing an understanding of and respect for difference.* Thirdly, *both indoor and outdoor environments should support interactions between children, and between children and adults.* (NCCA, 2004, pp. 54–55)

According to the European Commission Network on Childcare, 1996, the design and organisation of the physical environment should reflect the pedagogical philosophy of the service. Indeed it has also been suggested that the closer the match between arrangement of space and the pedagogical vision of a setting, the higher the quality of the ECEC setting (van Liempd & Hoekstra, 2007). In this chapter we explore the various meeting points between pedagogical vision and the design and resourcing of spaces for young children, also paying attention to key mediating factors including broader socio-historical, political and economic factors. The chapter begins by tracing how the design of early childhood learning environments has changed over time. Also considered is the relationship between learning environments and contextual factors such as regulations, institutional regimes, building regulations, perceptions of risk and safety and the desired visibility of children in public space. An ecological perspective of early learning environments is proposed as offering a useful framework for planning, designing and reviewing the physical environments indoors and outdoors where learning takes place.

The relationship between pedagogical vision and design of space: a view from the past

Questions around the optimum physical environment for young children's learning have demanded attention of prominent early childhood educators for centuries. As noted in Chapter 2, at the onset of industrialisation in the late eighteenth century the preferred environment for young children's education was considered to be the rural one where they would be protected from the perceived chaos and corruption of cities. Rousseau exhorted, 'Send your children to renew themselves, so to speak; send them to regain in the open fields the strength lost in the foul air of our crowded cities' (Rousseau, 1762, 130). Beginning in the early nineteenth century, particular educational philosophies and methodologies began to be expressed in terms of quite specific guidelines regarding the design and organisation of the indoor and outdoor environment, as well as in the kinds of materials, objects, activities and opportunities young children should be provided with. Reference was also often made to the optimum physical location of an ECEC setting in a community, as well as its interface with that community.

When Friedrich Froebel was asked in 1833 to devise a plan for the education of the poor in Willisau, in the canton of Berne in Switzerland, he recommended that adults be actively involved in the children's play, both guiding and instructing. Thus, in contrast to the walled separate playgrounds in Wilderspin's infant schools, referred to in Chapter 2, Froebel recommended appropriately large playgrounds 'close and in living relationship with people's lives' (Lilley, 1967, p. 168). Some years later, when the first kindergarten opened in Bad Blankenburg, a town nested in Thuringin forests, Froebel continued to stress the togetherness of adults and children at play (Heiland, 1993) in the provision of circle games, and areas for parents and other visitors to observe the activities of the kindergarten. It is also worth noting that the curriculum for young children based on play arose in the context of specifically German prohibitions against academic learning (reading, writing, number work) in preschool institutions (Taylor Allen, 2000). Froebel devised a series of materials – *Gifts* and *Occupations* – which he viewed as meeting children's activity and occupational drive. There were six *Gifts* containing a variety of items – from coloured woollen balls to wooden cubes that could be broken down in size and shape. Among other things, the *Occupations* included flat geometrical coloured tiles, sticks for stick-laying and interlacing, drawing, point-pricking, weaving, paper-folding and modelling using clay.

The underlying principles of his educational philosophy: life-unity with God, humanity and nature and harmonious community living, were reflected in the order of the *Gifts* and *Occupations*, their relatedness with the movement/circle games, as well as the physical design of the outdoor space. When Schrader-Breymann, Froebel's niece, founded a kindergarten and teacher-training programme in Berlin in 1872, she urged the kindergarten trainees to understand children in the context of the urban society in which they lived. She abandoned aspects of Froebelian education she regarded as too abstract and philosophical such as the movement games. However, because she regarded the estrangement of the city child from nature as unnatural, she designed specific exercises to acquaint children with the natural environment, the adult world and the skills of everyday life (Taylor Allen, 2000).

Early infant schools in the British Isles had quite a different architectural design and pedagogical vision. They were designed to accommodate very large numbers of young children and to maintain social order in cities. The Model Infant School in Marlborough Street, Dublin, which was constructed between 1836 and 1838, comprised one large schoolroom in which the large number of children was subdivided into 12 smaller groups, each under the eye of a monitor (an older, more advanced pupil). The layout of the room combined the Lancasterian system (rows of parallel desks), named after the English educator Joseph Lancaster (1778–1839), with a raised gallery that could accommodate a large group of children. While older children were taken to do group work in the three smaller classrooms, younger children had lessons while seated in the gallery. School registers from its first year of operation in 1838 indicated an attendance of 64 boys and 62 girls. By 1840, numbers had reached a peak of 422 boys and 283 girls.

Apart from the Infant Model School, little attention was paid to the design of the school environment of the 4,000 plus national schools built around Ireland in the middle decades of the nineteenth century as part of the expansion of a national system of primary education (O'Dwyer, 1992). Nevertheless the following excerpt from *The Irish Builder* in 1890 suggests that some attention to detail was paid to architectural details in some schools:

> *The first stone of a new school for infants was laid yester-day by the Hon. The Recorder. Its site is on Arbour-hill, near the Garrison Church. The building is to be known as 'The Victoria Kindergarten School' and will comprise a principal schoolroom, 40 ft by 20ft, with a classroom, 10ft by 10ft. At one end of the school room there will be a 'gallery', capable of accommodating 100 infants. Red brick of best quality will be used for the external facing, and internally the roof will be sheeted with pitch pine stained and varnished.* (*The Irish Builder*, Notes of Works, 15 April 1890).

The inclusion of a gallery designed for passive rote learning in the spatial layout in this 'kindergarten school' is at odds with Froebel's original intention of a place of self-directed activity. A further interesting dimension of the design of such buildings, which is found in the design of infant schools in general at the early stages of mass compulsory education, is the relationship between school architecture and social control. This issue has been the focus of analysis by educational historians who have commented on school architecture in relation to discourses of control, surveillance, conformity, compliance and resistance (Margolis & Fram, 2007). It has also drawn comment from sociologists of children with respect to more recent school architecture (some sociologists have applied a Foucaultian analysis by framing ECEC and school settings as sites of governance and control (McNaughton, 2005; Devine, 2003)). Describing the manner in which the spatial organisation of many contemporary primary school settings can control and regulate children's behaviour, James *et al.* comment:

> *Children can be placed in rows, classes can be broken down into tables or groups and specialized into activities, individuals can be put in the 'reading corner', required to stand by teacher's table or come out to front. Everyone can be evacuated, that is, sent out to exercise in the playground.* (James *et al.* 1998, p.45)

A small-scale research study conducted by Kernan in 1989, which compared classroom layout and pedagogical approaches of reception class/junior infant teachers in eight primary schools in Dublin and London, reported more opportunities for choosing, freer independent access to materials and activities, and freer movement around the classroom in the experience of the London children compared to their Dublin peers, where, by and large, the teacher directed where and with whom the children sat, as well as controlling children's movement in the classroom for most of the day (Kernan, 1989). Almost 20 years later the dominance of teacher-directed learning and whole-class teaching in Irish infant classrooms drew critical comment from the authors of the *OECD Thematic Review of ECE* (OECD, 2004). The report also noted the lack of attention to and skills concerning ECEC design.

In contrast to short time periods of adult-directed learning, with outdoor play times for recovery, which characterised the first infant schools, and, it could be argued, infant education in Ireland throughout the twentieth century, the nursery school pedagogical vision that emerged from the work of Rachel and Margaret McMillan in England was built upon a belief that freedom, opportunity, self-chosen activities and co-operative activity would encourage creativity, learning and education for citizenship (de Lissa, 1937). A central pathway to such learning was through play. Improving the health of working-class children living in poor housing conditions in southeast London was the primary concern of the McMillan sisters in their early projects.

In her book, *The Nursery School*, first published in 1919,

Margaret McMillan provided detailed information regarding the specific role different elements of the design and resourcing were perceived to have in the nurture and education of young, working-class children. In the early years of their development, McMillan conceived the nursery garden schools as open-air nursery schools. She described the nursery buildings as 'shelters'. 'We have ample evidence to show that even very weak children recover health and begin to thrive only when they get away from enclosures and walls, and are allowed to live – with reasonable safeguards, of course, in the open. The great Healer is in the sky' (McMillan, n.d.) These 'shelters' were provided for different age groups with the intention that the children of different ages would 'meet often as in a family, in the gardens, at playtime, in visits to each other's shelters' (p.14). The nursery buildings should face south or southeast, with 'walls at either end shaped in butterfly form to catch all the sunshine possible' (p.15). Each child should have his own locker and shelf. All materials were physically accessible to the children. The outdoor space, envisaged as a nursery garden, was designed to provide opportunities for sensory stimulation and physically active play and challenge. Terraces, low walls, stones, steps and pathways were included to encourage 'muscular play and action'. The environment thus included jumping-off places and apparatuses that, according to McMillan 'will provoke children not only to play, but to play bravely and adventurously' (McMillan, 1930, p. 28). Like Froebel, McMillan was also keen that that the activities in the nursery garden could be observed by adults, particularly by mothers (McMillan, 1930; Steedman, 1990). McMillan also proposed 'covered ways' linking the surrounding houses to the nursery (p.16).

The early educator probably most associated with attention to the design of the physical environment is Maria Montessori. A core concept in her scientific pedagogy first realised in the *Casa dei Bambini* (Children's House) in the housing project of San Lorenzo in Rome was the 'the prepared environment'. The prepared environment has generally come to be associated with the defined 'areas' of a Montessori classroom: practical life, sensorial, maths, language, geography, science, art and music. Each area contained specific materials, the design of which, their order and intended use were derived from Montessori's observations of children's natural learning dispositions and engagement with the environment. Concepts and observations highlighted and revisited by Montessori in her many publications and lectures included: children's spontaneous interest and activity, concentration and involvement; engagement with all the senses; love of repetition, order and silence; preference for freedom of choice in activity; importance of independent access to the environment; and the necessity of movement (Standing, 1957). Consequently, the materials in the Montessori classroom were (and continue to be) designed to be physically accessible, attractive, simple and natural. Many also included control of error (i.e. they are self-correcting) in their design, providing children with feedback and facilitating independent learning (Stoll Lillard, 2005).

Although there is no definitive blueprint for the design and layout of a Montessori school building, Montessori discussed aspects of the broader physical design and how it affected children's learning in many of her books and articles. For example, she paid attention to the physical and visual connectedness between the indoors and outdoors and highlighted the importance of children both having low windows to look out through and attention to what they can see outdoors. She also recommended that the outdoor space should be 'in direct communication with the schoolroom, so that the children may be free to go and come as they like, throughout the entire day' (Montessori, 1964, pp. 80–81). Montessori also felt that it was important that children had the possibility of regulating the colour and the degree of light in the environment. Darkness for example, supported those moments when 'perfect silence and immobility' was desired. The provision of cosy corners were advised to allow the children the possibility to isolate him/herself and be alone (AMI, personal communication, December 2004).

An application of Montessori's essential ideas in an urban environment is evident in Lili Peller's *Haus der Kinder* (Children's House) in Vienna in the 1930s. Peller was a close friend of Montessori's and she collaborated with architect Franz Schuster on the design. Peller points to the necessity of teachers becoming interested in housing design. This would help them arrange spaces that children could explore, understand and use and where their private initiative and personal responsibility would be preserved. Particular design features referred to by Peller included: having windows that children can look through; direct connections to the outdoor space from the indoors; providing an unobstructed view from inside out and vice versa; and a cluster arrangement of rooms, with the main room in the centre and direct access to smaller, satellite rooms, including a quiet room. Peller also refers to the qualities of space that are most meaningful to young children – the feeling of spaciousness or nestling in a small enclosure – and thus recommends the inclusion of alcoves and nooks (Peller, 1996). Interestingly, many of Montessori's and McMillan's ideas about the design and qualities of space find resonance in contemporary design and resourcing recommendations for ECEC.

Collaboration between designers, educators and children: a contemporary view

In recent years architecture and landscape design and environmental psychology are increasingly being applied in ECEC design and there are growing numbers of collaborative projects between architects, pedagogues and planners (Burgard, 2000; Clark, 2005; Dudek, 2001; Greenman, 2005; Gulløv, 2003; National Children's Nurseries Association, 2002). A further development is the participation of users, including children and parents, in the planning stages of such projects. In part this reflects the growing cross-disciplinary work in childhood studies and the 'philosophy of listening' discussed in Chapter 3. It may also be viewed as part of the wider developments in urban regeneration across Europe that favours an integrated and inclusive approach in the provision of services (URBACT, EU), and the active participation of children, families and local organisations from planning through to implementation.

However, it is also recognised that ECEC settings have become an increasingly significant site of young children's daily lives as children worldwide are spending more time in out-of-home settings. As more children avail of ECEC, the importance of quality ECEC, both in providing children with a good start in life and as an overall 'public good', is increasingly recognised nationally and internationally (Department for Health and Children, 2000; National Council for Curriculum and Assessment (NCCA), 2004; Organisation for Economic Co-operation and Development (OECD), 2006; Shonkoff & Phillips, 2000). The outcome of these developments is that more attention is being paid to designing meaningful and inclusive spaces for children and families and a shared vocabulary between educators, designers and users is slowly beginning to emerge.

When the European Commission Childcare Network published *Quality Targets in Services for Young Children* in 1996, it became a benchmark for subsequent developments in ECEC at a European level. A number of targets referred specifically to the provision of space. 'Space is liberty,' wrote the authors. 'The freedom to explore their environment inside and outside, to move freely, and to have sufficient rest, is important for the motor, social and intellectual development of young children' (p.26). The authors also remarked on the wide variation across European countries in attention to design of ECEC environments. In some countries they noted, 'the physical environment of nurseries has become a matter of architectural, design and planning interest (Denmark and Italy were cited in this regard), in other countries ... buildings are strictly functional, poorly fabricated or inadequately converted from other uses ... the need for security in some vandalised areas is regarded as precluding aesthetic – or any other considerations' (European Commission Childcare Network, 1996, p. 26).

By and large, Ireland has not been recognised as a country with a tradition of good design for children. While attention to design is slowly beginning to increase, the approach appears to be cautious and lacking in ambition, perhaps reflecting the low base Ireland is coming from in terms of design and construction of spaces for children and the ambiguous view regarding children's status and their visibility in the community and in public space. Recognising the contribution the learning environment makes to good-quality ECEC, Standard 2 of *Síolta – The National Quality Framework for Early Childhood Education* is as follows:

> *Enriching environments, both indoor and outdoor (including materials and equipment) are well maintained, safe, available, accessible, adaptable, developmentally appropriate, and offer a variety of challenging and stimulating experiences* (CECDE, 2006).

One of the strategies that has been utilised to promote good design in spaces for children worldwide has been the organisation of architectural competitions in ECEC. In 1985 the city authorities in Frankfurt commissioned a programme of thirty-five new ECEC settings (kindergartens). Generous funding was provided in recognition of the place of the kindergarten as a public institution that signified contemporary life and living (Penn, 2000). A key part of the design specification was that the architecture should appeal directly to children. The buildings also had to complement the local surroundings:

> *The quality of the architecture must be directed towards children. The structural space should support the children in their social learning as well as in their sensory learning. By adapting the premises to the powers of sensory perception, a sense of spatial awareness should be transmitted ... the contemporary kindergarten architect risks taking up the*

challenge of play. His spatial play should harmonise with the children's play (Burgard, 2000, p.90).

Twenty years later, in 2005, *Children in Europe* (a European network formed to exchange ideas and experiences in the field of ECEC), in collaboration with the OECD and the Royal Incorporation of Architects in Scotland, held an international competition in architecture and design for young children, which attracted entries from seventeen countries worldwide (Children in Scotland, 2006). A common theme across all the award-winning entries was the fact that the designs were both in tune with the local landscape (context-sensitive) and with how children want to use their space. These two factors are clearly articulated in the evolving and dynamic designs of the ECEC settings in the Reggio Emilia area of Northern Italy.

The educational significance of space: a view from Reggio Emilia

From the outset, and under the guidance of Loris Malaguzzi (1920–1994) and the teachers and pedagogues he worked with, the environment of the Reggio Emilia schools was conceived as a fully participating element in education and the educational significance of space was appreciated (Gandini, 1998). Over the years since the approach was first conceived, architects and designers have collaborated with the schools' teams in the search for greater harmony between the spaces (indoors and outdoors) and the pedagogical philosophies and methods, as well as the ever-changing cultural and organisation needs (Vecchi, 1998). The environment is portrayed as flexible and living, undergoing frequent modification by children and teachers in order to remain responsive to their needs (Gandini, 1998). As community-based concerns and responsibilities, Reggio Emilia schools are located at the centre of a neighbourhood, physically and metaphorically. The daily lives of children and teachers are envisioned as 'a visible point of reference for the community' (Gandini, 1998, p.164), and the spaces surrounding the schools are considered extended classroom space (Gandini, 1998). A key design element of the schools is transparency. Indoors, this takes the form of glass walls and windows. Transparency towards the outside (Rinaldi, 1998) is also applicable, where a symbiotic relationship between the outside and inside is prioritised.

During the 1990s a collaborative project was initiated between Reggio children and architects and designers of the Domus Academy Research Centre on designing spaces for children. The output of this collaboration represents a critical analysis of the cumulative experience of Reggio Emilia in the identification of desirable characteristics and reflections on design for spaces for young children (Ceppi & Zini, 1998). A key question posed at the outset of the project was: 'what kind of space do children need in order to inhabit a school in the best way?' (Vecchi, 1998). Beginning by noting that there are alternative ways (from the traditional) of designing spaces, the authors write of spaces that are 'softer, less rigid, more open to the indeterminableness of ex-perience' (Ceppi & Zini, 1998). The metaphor of *osmosis* is evoked to capture the close relationship between the school and the town and city, as well as the strong relationship between the inside and the outside of the building. The authors identify the importance for children to feel in harmony with the environment outside the school and to be aware of the changes taking place:

> *A school should be a place that 'senses' what is happening outside – from the weather to seasonal changes, from the time of day to the rhythms of the town – precisely because it exists in a specific place and time* (Ceppi & Zini, 1998, p.41).

Particular reference is made to the use of natural light as a design tool, noting both the biological necessity of light for life and the fact that a large quantity of natural light enables us to 'sense' the outside. Specific design elements described and illustrated that foster this inside-outside relationship include:

- *'filter' spaces (porches, verandas, canopies)*
- *conservatories and interior courtyards (open or covered), with plants and other natural elements;*
- *the particular use of the outdoor spaces: hillocks, play equipment, pathways, specially equipped areas;*
- *installations for making visible the behaviour of physical forces (e.g. wind, water); and*
- *an entrance that provides information on the school and its activities, a place for welcoming and greetings* (Ceppi & Zini, 1998, pp.97–107).

The cultural and physical context within which these recommendations were made are the highly urbanised regions of Northern Italy, with consequential noise pollution, high levels of traffic and toxic fumes. In this respect, reference is also made to the use of vegetation as both a barrier to noise and air pollution and as a didactic tool. One of the key metaphors referred to by Ceppi & Zini, 1998 captures the interaction of space, time and place referred to in Chapter 3. This is 'overall softness', meaning an 'eco-system that is diversified, stimulating and welcoming, where each inhabitant is part of a group but also has spaces for privacy and a pause from the general rhythms' (Ceppi & Zini, 1998).

Children's perspectives on various elements of the design of spaces in schools in Reggio Emilia and what is important for them are revealed in a pamphlet entitled 'Advisory', prepared by the five- and six-year-olds at Diana Municipal Preschool in Reggio Emilia for three-year-olds who are about to enter. This excerpt captures the importance of placeness, belonging and feeling secure, whilst also having the opportunities for risk and challenge.

There are two small gardens inside the school. We call them gardens of beauty. They show some things of nature. You can see the sky and trees come out of the roof. ...The sunlight gets in through the paintings we made ourselves on the window panes and makes them brilliant. If you are a little sad, you can take a look at the gardens and you'll cheer up. Outside there are two gates, a small one and a big one. The big one has no doorbell, and the small one has a push-button we just can't get to. You must climb a tree to make it. It's slippery and we think it's dangerous for a three-year-old child. You'd better wait till you are five. The tree house is up there, just before your eyes. You must be careful when you use it because if somebody moves too much on the rope bridge, he may fall. It's very adventurous. You feel very scared at first, then you get used to it. The little mountain in the backyard is just the best. You can let yourselves slide down with a pulley ... you can play at the secret house there. Do you know how? Take, you know, the cardboard that you see around and then play and do anything you want, even hide-and-seek (Bondavalli, Mori & Vecchi and children of Reggio Emilia, 1993).

By virtue of their specialised role as educators, individual early years practitioners can use their knowledge of children's interests and their learning dispositions to create ECEC environments that provide a wide range of possibilities and that promote learning and development, engender a feeling of security and well-being, and build a sense of community for the children in their care (Bruce, 1987; Hendricks, 2001; Rinaldi, 1998). However, it becomes clear that the pedagogical practices are, to a certain extent, 'inscribed outside the walls of a particular ECEC institution' (Kjørholt & Tingstad, 2007). They are influenced by a complex interconnected range of factors, including historical and cultural traditions and values; dominant political and economic discourses, locally and nationally; whether services are located within the formal education sector or within the care sector; the age to which early childhood curricula or guidelines are targeted; as well as regulatory frameworks (Abbott, 2001; Blenkin & Kelly, 1997; Bennett, 2005). An overriding concern in the development of new ECEC services in Ireland is the government's determination to increase the number of 'childcare places'. Often this appears to be more about the demands of the labour force rather than about children's interests in the here and now (Hayes, 2007). Children's and early years practitioners' voices can also become marginalised when dealing with the competing demands of the power of local politics, building regulations and costs and the real threat of vandalism.

School and preschool design considerations are bound by national building regulations. In recent decades in Ireland, they have also been heavily influenced by both the need to minimise accidents because of litigation, and by budgets and costs. The formal primary education sector has been dogged by delays in school building projects, while children are being accommodated in temporary prefabricated buildings for years on end, in overcrowded schools and, in some cases, having no access to school (Carr, 2007; Hayes, 2007). Over the years, changes in school architecture have had little to do with good design in spaces for children's environments. Rather they have largely been determined by more stringent fire and safety regulations. For example, the direct access to the outdoors from individual classrooms that became the norm in new school buildings constructed in Ireland since the 1970s was governed by fire regulations. The facilitation of direct indoor–outdoor access or indoor–outdoor connectedness from a pedagogical perspective was not part of the rationale for this development (personal communication, Senior Architect, Planning and Building Unit, Department of Education and Science, April 2005).

Supporting our understanding of children's spaces: cross-disciplinary theoretical perspectives

An increase in cross-disciplinary work has contributed to the emergence of new concepts, theories and ways of viewing children's interactions with the physical environments where they spend their time. Oftentimes 'new' concepts appear to be 'rediscoveries' of older concepts expressed in a different language. One such 'new' concept is the notion of children's spaces as porous rather than bounded (Ceppi & Zini, 1998; Holloway & Valentine, 2000), and connected to the communities in which they are located. The reciprocal and interdependent relationship between children and the physical environment is usefully captured in an ecological perspective, which has been referred to in Chapters 3 and 4 in relation to Bronfenbrenner's work. Newer concepts emerging include theoretical and practical interest in the relationship between space and place, and the notion of common spaces, 'placeness', identity and belonging (Moss & Petrie, 2002; Van Keulen, 2004; Singer & de Haan, 2007). These provide a useful reference point in ensuring ECEC settings are equitable spaces, fostering respect for diversity and social inclusion at a time when ECEC settings across Europe are characterised by growing heterogeneity. Let us first examine how an ecological perspective can support the creation and maintenance of content-rich environments.

Ecology is broadly concerned with organism interrelatedness or the mutual reciprocity between developing organisms and their environment (Shepard, 1969; Tudge, Gray & Hogan, 1997). It views the animal and the environment as an inseparable pair; one cannot exist without the other. One of the attractions of an ecological perspective in the present context is its meaningfulness to children's everyday lives. At its most fundamental level, children, as humans, thrive to the extent that they can get both meaning and value from their encounters with their surroundings (Reed, 1996), whether at home or in an early childhood education (ECEC) setting. Viewing early childhood education environments through an ecological lens helps focus our attention on the extent to which ECEC environments are rich in meaning and value for all children and families with the support of early years practitioners in feeling a sense of belonging, connecting to and knowing the world. Thus, it is important to consider the perspectives of all the users of space: babies, toddlers, young children, older children, parents and teachers.

One useful concept, which has been utilised by researchers coming from an ecological perspective seeking to understand children's encounters in their everyday worlds, is that of *affordance*. This concept is increasingly being utilised within ECEC research to describe the relationship between children and their settings. The term *affordance* was originally coined by perception psychologist James Gibson (1979) and explained as follows: *the affordances of the environment are what it offers* [an individual] ... *what it provides or furnishes, either for good or ill* (Gibson, 1979, p. 127). Affordance implies the complementarity of the individual and the environment. It refers to the perceived and actual properties of physical resources in the environment (fixed features of physical structure, objects and tools) and how they are used. One of the first researchers to utilise Gibson's concept of affordance in describing children's encounters with the physical environment was Heft (1988). He proposed a functional taxonomy of children's outdoor environments, which subsequently became influential amongst some play environment designers and researchers. Heft's taxonomy comprised ten categories as follows: (1) flat, relatively smooth surface; (2) relatively smooth slope; (3) graspable/detached object; (4) attached object; (5) non-rigid, attached object; (6) climbable feature; (7) aperture (admitting light); (8) shelter; (9) moldable material (e.g. dirt, sand); and (10) water. Each category was further defined in terms of its affordances. For example, 'shelter' affords microclimate, prospect, refuge, privacy. Moldable material affords construction of objects, pouring and modification of its surface features. The value of such an approach was that it offered a way of thinking about environments that was fundamentally active and goal directed (Heft, 1988) and which supported children's activity, curiosity, exploration and creativity. This is captured in Anita Rui Olds' recommendation that it is advisable is to conceive of all elements of the room (floors, walls, ceilings, horizontal and vertical supports, objects, forms and architectural details) as interactive surfaces when designing for 'richness' in children's spaces, *'The trick is to stop thinking in terms of standard definitions of walls, furniture and play objects and to start thinking in terms of the movements and activities children enjoy'* (Olds, 1988, p. 219).

Another more recent focus of interest which has drawn on the theory of affordances has been the examination of affordances in the context of the socio-cultural world, including the analysis of the diversity of potential affordances available to children in different contexts and the degree to which they are actualised, promoted or constrained (by adults) (Kernan, 2006; Kytta, 2002, 2004; Reed, 1996). Kernan's study examined children's experiences of the outdoor environment in ECEC settings in terms of extending spheres of experience (Kernan, 2006). This fundamental construct that has been utilised to describe how children perceive and understand the world is evident in the writing of some of the so-called 'pioneers' of early childhood education referred to earlier. It is also evident in Gibson and Pick's (2000) theory of perceptual learning and Reed's (1996) concept of fields of 'free' and 'promoted' action, extended by Kytta (2004) with reference to independent mobility. Tuan's (1977) description of human lives in terms of a dialectic movement between shelter and venture, attachment and freedom is also relevant.

Space, meaning room and scope for movement, is often associated with freedom and is 'longed for'. Place, on the other hand, means security and often the notion of being 'attached to' place is expressed. According to Tuan (1977), space and place require each other and humans require both. From the security and stability of place, there is an awareness of openness, freedom and, sometimes, threat of space.

In Kernan's study, extending fields of action are conceptualised in three interconnected fields: indoor–outdoor connectedness, boundaried outdoor space, and the wider outdoors.

Indoor–outdoor connectedness considers transparency between indoors and outdoors at a number of levels. These include: the visibility of the setting to the community and the community to the setting; children of all ages and abilities being able to perceive affordances for action and change and novelty outdoors while indoors; ease of movement between indoors and outdoors; being able to bring indoors out, and outdoors in. Implicated in this field is attention to design of the transition points between indoors and outdoors (i.e. windows, doorways, entrances, exits).

The next sphere of experience considers the *boundaried outdoor space* of an ECEC setting. Of interest here are the potential affordances for action for children of different ages, stages of development and abilities, girls and boys and the extent to which they are supported or constrained by pedagogical and regulatory practices. Thus consideration of surface layout (Gibson 1979), the amount of space available, naturally occurring and designed features such as different levels, availability of loose parts, transformable materials, pathways and small spaces are also relevant in this sphere of action. A further consideration in this field is the degree of comfort for children and adults, a factor that also implies attention to design – in particular, orientation and sun path, and the possibilities for shelter.

The third and final sphere of experience incorporates consideration of *the wider outdoors* beyond the boundaried area of the ECEC setting where children are clearly visible to the wider community. Here, the immediately accessible neighbourhood, including pathways, green spaces, parks, 'wilderness' spaces and other public and community spaces, and the range of physical features and social contacts therein, are of significance. As in the other fields, affordances for action and the extent to which they are promoted or constrained are also considered. One of the propositions of the study was that children's opportunities to perceive and actualise affordances outdoors was dependent on the design of the physical environment, whether adults facilitated access to the outdoors and on the environment children encountered once outdoors. This encompassed design, topology, size of space, availability of loose parts and the extent to which adults permitted mobility and facilitated individual children's strivings to explore.

A characteristic of all four ECEC settings in this ethnographic study was the invisibility of young children in the public space of the community, and of the community and the outside world to children. This was due to a range of interrelated structural factors including a lack of resources; the tendency to prioritise indoor environment over the outdoors; a lack of awareness of and attention to building design features permitting transparency between indoors and outdoors; a tension between regulatory and institutional requirements and children's needs and priorities; fear of vandalism and litigation; and the dominance of car traffic over the needs of the playing young child. The net result was that it was difficult for children to 'sense' the outdoors while indoors and to perceive and utilise affordances outdoors. Furthermore, time and space to play outdoors was often severely limited. Thus the frequency and duration of play opportunities outdoors, and the possibilities to forge connections with and understand the surrounding world in a meaningful way, were reduced.

Tuan's (1977) work has foregrounded the importance of understanding human dispositions, capacities, needs and feelings in relation to physical settings. Applied to this study, it became apparent that environments outdoors that young children enjoyed most were often the places where adults enjoyed being with children. There, adults were more relaxed, relationships with children more fluid, and adults were more likely to wish to spend extended periods of time there and consequently children too. Both adults and children were observed to share in delight and discovery of observing change outdoors. When not overly stressed by organisational and regulatory requirements, adults and children enjoyed venturing forth in small groups, to the spatial expansiveness of walks and exploration of the wider outdoors and then returning to the familiarity and security of the ECEC setting. However, the richness or value of the experience that made it rewarding for both children and adults depended on a number of contingent factors, including: adults' intuitive understanding of children; their listening to and engagement with children's questions; a willingness to engage in playful, sometimes adventurous activity; to be in tune with what was fun and interesting for children, and group size. In this respect, it seemed important for adults to be in touch with their own memories of a sensing and playful childhood, with children's rhythms of play, and be able to put aside the sometimes excessive seriousness of the pressure of accountability, professionalism and order without losing sight of children's need for responsible and trustworthy adults.

A committed, well-trained and supported staff has been identified internationally as the most essential element of early childhood programme quality and positive experiences for children (Burchinal, Cryer, Clifford & Howes, 2002; NESF, 2005; Weiss, 2005). It is useful to reflect critically on the interaction between the early years practitioner, the design of the learning environment on the one hand, and 'good' ECEC and positive experiences for children on the other hand. Victor Sidy, an architectural design consultant to Montessori schools in the United States, remarks that when he began to formulate a paper which he hoped would demonstrate that good architecture makes good Montessori education, he was persistently haunted by instances of remarkable education occurring in spaces he had classified as substandard, with poor quality of light, limited space and bad acoustics. He also noted that whilst he might design an 'intelligent, sensitive building', the building also needed inspired teaching (Sidy, 2003). In her recommendations regarding ECEC learning environments, Fisher (2002) highlights design, space and time dimensions as well as access to adults. She writes that ECEC learning environments should provide the following elements:

- *new and interesting experiences;*
- *activities that encourage children's natural curiosity;*
- *opportunities to explore, experiment and become competent;*
- *a timetable that is sufficiently flexible to give the children some control over when and how experiences/activities/tasks are carried out;*
- *learning that occurs in a range of contexts – the classroom, outside of the classroom, on visits, on trips, in workplaces, in the street; and*
- *access to adults and other expert and experienced people (including other children) who will answer and raise questions and pose challenges to extend learning and understanding* (Fisher, 2002, p.77).

When Sidy (2003) sought to identify the elements of the Montessori approach to education that were missing from the typical architecture discourse, the notion of 'nurturing buildings' emerged, understood as:

> *Buildings that relate to the land and surrounding nature; buildings that respond to the solar cycle of the day and the cycle of the seasons; buildings with a purpose of caring, sheltering their users; buildings that are born of community interaction and buildings that, in their materials and structure, can teach lessons* (Sidy, 2003, pp.147–148).

Sidy's reference to nurturing, caring and shelter in school building design requires further elaboration in the context of contemporary

ECEC. Two questions arise: firstly, how can ECEC environments engender feelings of security and belonging, both of which are fundamental prerequisites of learning in ECEC settings? Secondly, how can we ensure that all children derive benefits from ECEC environments where they spend a large proportion of their day?

How can spaces for children become places to belong?

As a general principle, place identity requires a sense of ownership, attachment and familiarity with the ECEC environment. This results in a sense of security and belonging which in turn gives children the confidence needed to explore and challenge themselves (Trancik & Evans, 1995). This applies to all children, and indeed to adults. However, it may be even more important for children and families who are 'different' and who, as a result of such difference, whether due to culture, language, economic status or ability, may struggle to feel a sense of belonging and security. Good practice in ECEC indicates a proactive role for early years practitioners with respect to diversity and social inclusion (Derman-Sparks, 1989; French, 2003; Nutbrown, 1996). In order to create places to belong, particular attention needs to be paid to aspects of the physical and social environment. This involves incorporating familiar characteristics into the ECEC setting, paying particular attention to making entrance areas welcoming and reflecting all children's backgrounds and abilities in the design, resourcing and images displayed in ECEC environments.

Ensuring that ECEC spaces are safe is also a fundamental principle of good practice in ECEC (French, 2003) and early years practitioners, without exception, should never lose sight of their responsibilities always to ensure the safety of the children in their care. However, a number of writers have pointed to the fact that ECEC settings are being constrained by increased regulation of children's environments where fear of insurance claims, litigation and meeting the requirements of the regulatory authorities appear to be overriding concerns (Adams, 2006; Factor, 2004). Moss (2005) analyses the increasing tendency to regulate young children's activities within the context of a broader regulatory trend that has become stronger in the last thirty years as the world has come to seem more threatening and competitive, less orderly and controllable. One consequence of the increased emphasis on the avoidance of risk is to limit *the very sorts of experiences long held to be part of a healthy and happy early childhood* (New, Mardell & Robinson, 2005). Meeting children's need for risk is also complicated in settings that cater for children in a wide age range. What may be physically challenging, interesting and risky for a two-year-old may not provide four-year-olds with sufficiently satisfying or physically challenging experiences.

One approach taken demonstrates how risk-taking is a developmental necessity, i.e. essential to growing up, a natural part of being a child and related to encountering the unknown – feelings of competency, gaining confidence and independence (Greenman, 2005; Moorcock, 1998; Smith, 1998; Stephenson, 2003). The congruity of pedagogical vision, design and safety also needs attention. Thus it is important that when independence is encouraged it is complemented with safe design (Trancik & Evans, 1995). The guidelines from High/Scope with regard to creating learning environments provide a good model in this respect (Hohmann & Weikart, 2002). Another recommendation is that potentially dangerous activities that need plenty of supervision should be placed in close proximity to one another and not be interspersed with relatively safe activity pockets. Creating clusters of space needing high levels of supervision will optimise the teacher's energies and allow children maximum autonomy in areas where minimum supervision is required (Trancik & Evans, 1995).

Talking about the space can generate discussion about an individual ECEC setting's pedagogical vision and the degree to which it communicates belonging and security. Points of reflection and discussion might include the following:

- *Is it important for groups of same-age children to have a separate secure base/room? What is the desired level of interaction between children of different age groups, and how does the space layout facilitate this?*
- *Are there distinct spaces for different kinds of activities and are there clear pathways between them?*
- *Can children see other activity areas and move independently from one to another?*
- *Can children move independently from indoors to outdoors?*
- *Are there sufficient different play/activity areas indoors and outdoors for the numbers of children, keeping in mind children's preference to play in small groups (2 to 5 children)?*
- *Is there sufficient challenge, and complexity in the space and activities provided indoors and outdoors?*
- *Is there sufficient choice, or perhaps too much choice, in the activities and materials provided?*
- *Are there possibilities for privacy and restorative places?*
- *Is there a balance between quiet and 'busy' or noisy areas?*
- *Is it considered important to be able to bring materials and resources from indoors to the outdoors and from the outdoors to the indoors, and how does the design, layout and resources support this if desired?*
- *Can children easily find and independently access a wide range of materials and equipment?*
- *Is there sufficient coherence and legibility in the environment?*
- *How does the design of the environment support children to connect with the local community and landscape?* (adapted from van Liempd & Hoekstra, 2007; Trancik & Evans, 1995).

ECEC settings with a mixture of square, straight and curvy indoor spaces and flat, inclined, rough and smooth floors, along with a variety of outdoor terrain, have greater potential for complexity. Mystery also contributes to complexity by offering the prospect of discovering new objects and places (Trancik & Evans, 1995). Colour, natural light, acoustics, aesthetics, furnishing, entrance area, how the children's work and activities are documented and displayed, orientation and connectedness to the community and the surrounding built and natural landscape: all these elements communicate messages about the particular vision of an ECEC setting and need careful consideration from the perspective of all the users of an ECEC setting (children, parents and early years practitioners) (French, 2003; NCNA, 2002; van Liempd & Hoekstra, 2007).

SUMMARY

This chapter provided a wide-ranging view of ECEC learning environments, drawing on perspectives from history of education, architecture, psychology and ecology. The aim has been to explore different ways of thinking about the design and resourcing of physical space indoors and outdoors. The chapter considers the importance of the 'match' between pedagogical vision and the arrangement of space; the need to think about ECEC design from the perspectives and preferences of all the users, children and adults; the importance of engaging with how young children of different ages use and interact with space and all the physical features of the environment; viewing indoor and outdoor spaces as interconnected and in harmony with each other and with the surrounding environment and community and, finally, the importance of spaces which engender feelings of security and belonging and which offer children opportunities for risk and challenge.

Points for reflection

Drawing on the ecological stance proposed in this chapter, think about an early childhood education and care setting you are familiar with. How does the design and arrangement of the physical space support all children to inhabit that space and feel a sense of security and belonging? What aspects of physical design contribute to the setting being in harmony with the surrounding landscape and community?

Chapter eight

Changing the Landscape of Early Childhood Education and Care

INTRODUCTION

Children are the social group most affected by the quality of early childhood services. While this seems like a truism, there is a relative complacency apparent in Ireland about what actually happens children in their everyday experiences and an assumption that by just attending early years settings they will develop and progress positively. In fact the quality of everyday experiences in the early years – wherever children are – has a profound influence on them. They are not merely recipients or consumers of a service, but are deeply influenced, individually and collectively, by their early years experiences. The National Children's Strategy recognises that children affect and are affected by the environments within which they develop. They are active participants in our society and have a right to expect that early childhood settings will challenge and excite them, provide safety and security and enhance their overall development and learning. It is the intention of this book to review current understandings of how early childhood pedagogy impacts on children and to act as a stimulus for adults to reflect on their practice and the quality of provision for young children so that the experience of early childhood settings will be a positive and affirming one for all those involved.

The contexts

Children develop in the midst of many different and interacting systems. Whilst the family is recognised as the central space for early development, an increasing number of families share the early care and education of their children with various types of services. These services grow and are supported as part of the wider society and have, to a greater or lesser degree, contacts with other educational, social and cultural settings in the wider community. As such they provide an important bridge for children and parents alike, particularly useful where services are provided for minority or marginalised parents and their children. While focusing on the role of the practitioner, this book recognises the important potential of early childhood settings in creating these links across various sytems.

Within research the role of the early years setting in modern societies is under review. It is no longer simply seen as a safe place to have children minded while parents work. Rather, it is recognised as an influential institution for children, one where their rights and needs can be met in a way that recognises and respects them. Within such settings children have the opportunity to develop a sense of belonging beyond the immediate family group; a sense of contribution to a new social system. The quality of these opportunities can influence their sense of identity; the view they form of themselves. This reality places an obligation on adults to be alert to the immediate environment whilst at the same time remaining sensitive to the background experiences of children and the valuable contribution of such experiences, even for very young children.

The early years child

This book considers the development and learning of young children from birth through to the age of six. This period of life has been defined internationally as the first stage in education and addresses the practices that occur in a wide range of settings, from home-based services through to larger, centre-based services. The contemporary view of children as active agents in their learning informs the book; even the very youngest child contributes to the context and content of their own development. This is not to underestimate the dependence of the child or the very powerful, protective role of the adult. It does, however, challenge adults to reconsider practice and to take account of the rich and diverse nature of each child when planning early care and education, designing learning spaces and providing learning opportunities.

Viewing children as participants in the early childhood education process allows adults to work with children as well as provide for them. It provides a context within which children can be seen as contemporaries to be valued in the here and now. While it is important to consider the future, and practitioners are contributing to the foundations of future learning, it is the immediate, day-to-day experiences that are of most relevance; these are the experiences that matter. Children learn from the world around them, and the ordinary has the potential to be extraordinary. Certainly the adult can contribute in making the experience of the ordinary a rich learning experience by expanding children's language, thinking and understanding.

Children trust adults and look to them for protection and guidance. Children are motivated to learn, to seek meaning in their world and they expect that the adults they meet will assist them in this endeavour. They bring to the learning situation their own capabilities and will develop, through their experiences, the dispositions for learning that contribute to their overall success among their peers and in new social environments. The importance of developing positive or generative dispositions is discussed within the book and the responsibility of adults to reflect carefully on their practice is stressed. It is through their experiences with adults in the early years that children develop a sense of their place in the world and the role that both they and adults play. To make the most of the early years, children need adults who trust them; adults who are excited, inspired and challenged by the children they work with. The child becomes the centre of practice and the curriculum reflects that. This is well illustrated in the approaches to curriculum used in New Zealand and Reggio Emilia. While very different in their structure, both these approaches to practice view the child as strong and competent and see the adult in an enabling role rather than a custodial/protective or a didactic/instructional role. The child has a key role in the activities and the adults are engaged with and connected to the child's world.

The adult in practice

It is a central thesis of this book that adults actively include children in the experiences of the early years setting, that they engage with children, learning from them as well as enhancing the learning opportunities for them. This pedagogical approach is informed by a belief in the active nature of child development and includes the child as a partner in development. Reviewing the research on how young children develop and learn, even from the earliest age, supports the contention that the early years are a critical time for children. It is at this stage in their development that children come to understand their world. Their curiosity and desire for knowledge is evident in their play, their exploration, their questions and their behaviour. The adult has a valuable contribution to make in this regard. The extent to which practice is responsive to learning opportunities of even the most mundane activity – such as nappy-changing, transition from one space to the next or tidy-up time – will influence the quality of that experience for the child. Settings that recognise that learning is an ongoing process will engage children in the day-to-day activities, will include them in planning and will expect them to contribute. The challenges of this approach to practice are recognised. It is not sufficient to make a plan for the day and follow it; the dynamic and interactive nature of development requires that practitioners are responsive and reflective throughout their engagement with children. The planning necessary for quality early childhood education and care is in terms of creating learning opportunities in a risk-rich, content-rich and language-rich environments. Practice is most effective when it is relational and responsive to the child.

To inform practice, the book introduces the concept of a nurturing pedagogy, a style of practice that is explicit in engaging children, respecting them and integrating the learning opportunities provided across the care and education dimensions. The idea behind this approach to practice is that it builds on the individual capabilities and dispositions of the child within the social context. It is derived from the belief that it is the close interactions among children and between children and adults that drive development and learning. These close and important interactions have been called 'proximal processes' and have been characterised as the engines of development (Bronfenbrenner & Morris, 1998). Examples include feeding and comforting babies, playing with young children, facilitating child-to-child interactions, comforting those in distress, making plans, acquiring new knowledge and know-how. Responding to our understanding of early childhood development requires that we prioritise relationships and interactions over direct instruction and teaching as the cornerstone of early educational practice.

Early learning environments

The site for early learning is a key contributing factor to the early learning process. In attending to the process of learning, the curriculum and the practice in early years settings, the design, organisation and resourcing of the physical environments where learning takes place may be neglected. This topic is discussed with particular reference to children's interactions with the physical environments, indoors and outdoors, where they spend their time. The concept of affordances – which describes the relationship between children and their settings – is considered in some detail. Furthermore, mechanisms for including children in the organisation of settings are proposed. There are challenges to designing learning environments that are appealing to children, allow for indoor and outdoor experiences and are safe, whilst also providing necessary opportunities for exploration, play and risk-taking. Meeting children's need for risk is complicated in settings that cater for children in a wide age range. What may be interesting and risky for two-year-olds may not provide four-year-olds with sufficiently satisfying or physically challenging experiences. Once again the idea of creating a sense of belonging is stressed. To create places where children feel they belong, adults need to pay particular attention to aspects of the physical and social environment. This involves incorporating images and materials that are familiar to the children into the setting, paying particular attention to making entrance areas welcoming and reflecting all children's backgrounds and abilities.

CONCLUSION

As the landscape for children changes in Ireland, this book is intended to widen the discussion and debate about how best to provide rich and rewarding early childhood experiences for children in whatever setting they may be. The interactions between individual children, the adults in their lives and the various learning environments are critical spaces for learning and are explored in some detail. We know that adults, and their style of engagement, have a profound impact on the learning experiences of children and set the scene for their own sense of engagement with the world. We also know a great deal about how children develop and learn, and recognise that early childhood experiences are important to children in their day-to-day lives and into their future. With growing interest in investing and supporting early childhood, there will be more research and attention to how we provide for all our children in a way that maximises their potential.

We hope this book will contribute to improving and maintaining the quality of early childhood services in Ireland and be of benefit to practitioners so that they will continue to reflect on their practice and enhance the development and learning of the young children with whom they work.

Bibliography

Abbott, L. & Moylett, H. (eds.) (1999a) *Early Education Transformed – New Millennium Series* (London: Falmer Press).

Abbott, L. & Nutbrown, C. (eds.) (2001) *Experiencing Reggio Emilia: Implications for Preschool Provision* (Buckingham: Open University Press).

Abbott, L. (1994) 'Play is Ace! Developing Play in Schools and Classrooms' in J. Moyles (ed.) *The Excellence of Play* (Buckingham: Open University Press), pp. 76–87.

Abbott, L. (2001) 'Perceptions of Play – A Question of Priorities?' in L. Abbott & C. Nutbrown (eds.) *Experiencing Reggio Emilia* (Buckingham: Open University Press), pp. 8–20.

Adams, K. (2006) 'Does Learning and Teaching Involve Risk-taking?' Paper presented at the 2nd International Froebel Society Conference, Froebel College of Education, Sion Hill, Blackrock, Dublin, 29 June to 1 July 2006.

Alderson, P. (1995) *Listening to Children: Children, Ethics and Social Research* (London: Barnardos).

Alderson, P. (2000) *Young Children's Rights: Exploring Beliefs, Attitudes, Principles and Practice* (London: J. Kingsley).

Alderson, P. (2005) 'Children's Rights: A New Approach to Studying Childhood' in H. Penn (ed.) *Understanding Early Childhood: Issues and Controversies* (Maidenhead: Open University Press), pp. 127–141.

Ames, C. (1992) 'Classrooms: Goals, Structures and Student Motivation', *Journal of Educational Psychology*, 84, 3, pp. 61–71.

Anning, A. (1995) *A National Curriculum for the Early Years* (Buckingham: Open University Press).

Athey, C. (1990) *Extending Thought in Young Children: A Parent–Teacher Partnership* (London: Paul Chapman Publishing).

Ball, C. (1994) *Start Right: The Importance of Early Learning* (London: RSA).

Banks, R. (2000) *The Early Childhood Education Curriculum Debate: Direct Instruction vs. Child-Initiated Learning* (ERIC Digest. Campaign, IL: ERIC/ECCE: Clearinghouse on Elementary and Early Childhood Education).

Bennett, J. (2005) 'Curriculum Issues in National Policy-making', *European Early Childhood Education Research Journal*, 13 (2), pp. 5–23.

Bennett, N., Wood, L. & Rogers, S. (1997) *Teaching Through Play: Teachers' Theories and Classroom Practice* (Buckingham: Open University Press).

Bergen, D., Reid, R. & Torelli, L. (2001) *Educating and Caring for Very Young Children: The Infant/Toddler Curriculum* (New York: Teachers College Press).

Berk, L.E. & Winsler, A. (1995) *Scaffolding Children's Learning: Vygotsky and Early Childhood Education* (Washington DC: NAEYC).

Bickhard, M. (1992) 'Scaffolding and Self-scaffolding: Central Aspects of Development' in L. Winegar & L. Valsiner (eds.) *Children's Development Within Social Context: Vol.2 Research and Methodology* (Hillsdale NJ: Erlbaum), pp. 33–51.

Blakemore, S.J. & Frith, U. (2000) *The Implications of Recent Developments in Neuroscience for Research on Teaching and Learning* (London: Institute of Cognitive Neuroscience).

Blenkin, G.M. & Kelly, A.V. (1997) *Principles into Practice in Early Childhood Education* (London: Paul Chapman).

Bloom, B. (1981) *All our Children Learning* (NY: McGraw-Hill).

Bondavalli, M., Mori, M. & Vecchi, V. (eds.) and Children of Reggio Emilia (1993) 'Children in Reggio Emilia look at the School', *Children's Environments*, 10 (2), pp. 39–45, retrieved 10 March 2006 from http://www.colorado.edu/journals/cye/.

Bourdieu, P. (1993) *Sociology in Question* (London: Sage).

Bowman, B.T., Donovan, M.S. & Burns, M.S (eds.) (2001) *Eager to*

Learn: Educating our Preschoolers (Washington DC: National Academic Press).

Bredekamp, S. & Copple, C. (eds.) (1997) *Developmentally Appropriate Practice in Early Childhood Programmes,* revised edition (Washington DC: National Association for the Education of Young Children).

Bredekamp, S. (1987) *Developmentally Appropriate Practice in Early Childhood Programmes Serving Children from Birth through Age 8* (Washington, DC: National Association for the Education of Young Children).

Brehony, K.J. (2003) 'A "Socially Civilising Influence"? Play and the Urban "Degenerate"', *Paedagogica Historica,* 39, pp. 87–106.

Brennan, C. (2004) *Power of Play: A Play Curriculum in Action* (Dublin: IPPA, the Early Childhood Organisation).

Bronfenbrenner, U. & Morris, P. (1998) 'The Ecology of Developmental Processes' in W. Damon & R.M. Lerner (eds.) *Handbook of Child Psychology Volume 1: Theoretical Models of Human Development,* 5th edition (New York: John Wiley & Sons), pp. 993–1028.

Bronfenbrenner, U. (1979) *The Ecology of Human Development* (Massachusetts: Harvard University Press).

Bronfenbrenner, U. (1995) 'Developmental Ecology: Through Space and Time: A Future Perspective' in P. Moen, G.H. Elder, Jr and K. Luscher (eds.) *Examining Lives in Context: Perspectives on the Ecology of Human Development* (Washington, DC: American Psychological Association), pp. 619–647.

Bronson, M. B. (2001) *Self-regulation in Early Childhood: Nature and Nurture* (NY: Guildford Press).

Brown, Mac H. & Freeman, N.K. (2001) '"We Don't Play That Way at Preschool": The Moral and Ethical Dimensions of Controlling Children's Play' in S. Reifel & Mac H. Brown (eds.) *Early Education and Care and Reconceptualising Play – Advances in Early Education and Day Care,* Volume II (Oxford: Elsevier Science), pp. 259–274.

Bruce, T. (1987) *Early Childhood Education* (London: Hodder & Stoughton).

Bruce, T. (1991) *Time to Play in Early Childhood Education* (Sevenoaks: Hodder & Stoughton).

Bruce, T. (1996) *Helping Young Children to Play* (London: Hodder & Stoughton).

Bruce, T. (1997) 'Adults and Children Developing Play Together', *European Early Childhood Research Journal,* Vol. 5, 1, pp. 89–99.

Bruce, T. (2001) *Learning Through Play: Babies, Toddlers and the Foundation Stage* (London: Hodder and Stoughton).

Bruer, J. (1999) *The Myth of the First Three Years: A New Understanding of Early Brain Development and Lifelong Learning* (New York: The Free Press).

Bruner, J. (1996) *The Culture of Education* (Cambridge MA: Harvard University Press).

Bruner, J., Jolly, A. & Sylva, K. (1985) *Play – Its Role in Development and Evolution* (London: Penguin).

Burchinal, M., Cryer, D., Clifford, R. & Howes, C. (2002) 'Caregiver Training and Classroom Quality in Child Care Centers', *Applied Developmental Science,* 6(1), pp. 2–11.

Burgard, R. (2000) 'The Frankfurt Kindergartens' in H. Penn (ed.) *Early Childhood Services: Theory, Policy and Practice* (Buckingham: Open University Press), 90–102.

Burman, E. (1994) *Deconstructing Developmental Psychology* (London: Routledge).

Caldwell, B. (1989) 'All Day Kindergarten – Assumptions, Precautions and Over-generalisations', *Early Childhood Research Quarterly,* 4, pp. 261–326.

Cameron, C. (2004) 'Social Pedagogy and Care', *Journal of Social Work,* Vol. 4, No. 2, pp. 133 – 151.

Campbell, S. (1999) 'Making the Political Pedagogical in Early Childhood', *Australian Journal of Early Education,* Vol. 24, 4, pp. 21–26.

Cannella, G.S. (1997) *Deconstructing Early Childhood Education: Social Justice and Revolution* (New York: Lang).

Cannella, G.S. (1998) 'Early Childhood Education: A Call for the Construction of Revolutionary Images' in W. Pilar (ed.) *Curriculum: Towards New Identities* (London: Garland Publishing/Taylor and Francis).

Carr, J. (2007) School Accommodation Plan for North Dublin/East Meath/South Louth Area, INTO Press Release, accessed 25 January 2007: http://www.into.ie/ROI/Publications/PressReleases/2007/ School AccommodationPlanforNDublinEMeathSLouthArea250107/.

Carr, M. (1997) 'Persistence When it's Difficult: A Disposition to Learn for early Childhood', *Early Childhood Folio,* NZCER.

Carr, M. (1998) 'A Project for Assessing Children's Experiences in Early Childhood Settings', Paper presented to the 8th EECERA Conference at Santiago de Compostela, Spain.

Carr, M. (1999) 'Being a Learner: Five Learning Dispositions for Early Childhood', *Early Childhood Practice,* 1, 1, pp. 81–99.

Carr, M. (2001a) *Assessment in Early Childhood Settings: Learning Stories* (London: Paul Chapman Publishing).

Carr, M. (2001b) 'Ready, Willing and Able: Learning Dispositions for Early Childhood?', Paper presented at *Cultures of Learning: Risk, Uncertainty and Education* Conference, University of Bristol, 19–22 April.

Carr, M. (2002) 'Emerging Learning Narratives: A Perspective from Early Childhood Education' in G. Wells and G. Claxton (eds.) *Learning for Life in the 21st Century* (London: Blackwell Publishers).

Carswell, D. (2002) *Child's Play: An Exploration into the Quality of Childcare Processes* (Dublin: Irish Preschool Playgroups Association).

Ceci, S.J. (1990) *On Intelligence ... More or Less: A Bio-ecological Treatise on Intellectual Development* (Englewood Cliffs, NJ: Erlbaum).

Centre for Early Childhood Development and Education (CECDE) (2006), *Síolta – The National Quality Framework for Early Childhood Education* (Dublin: Centre of Early Childhood Development and Education).

Ceppi, G. & Zini, M. (eds.) (1998) *Children, Spaces, Relations: Metaproject for an Environment for Young Children* (Reggio Emilia: Reggio Children and Comune di Reggio Emilia).

Children in Scotland (2006) Making Space: Award-winning Designs for Young Children, accessed 11 September 2007: http://www.childreninscotland.org.uk/makingspace.

Christensen, P. & O'Brien, M. (2003) 'Children in the City: Introducing New Perspectives' in P. Christensen & M. O'Brien (eds.) *Children in the City: Home, Neighbourhood and Community* (London, Routledge Falmer), pp. 1–12.

Civics Institute of Ireland, Annual Reports, 1933, 1935, 1938, 1940–41, 1945–46, 1946–47 and other correspondence, records and documentation sourced in The National Archives, Bishop Street, Dublin and Dublin City Archives, Pearse Street, Dublin.

Clark, A., & Moss, P. (2001) *Listening to Young Children: The Mosaic Approach* (London: National Children's Bureau).

Clark, A. (2005) 'Listening to and Involving Children: A Review of Research and Practice', *Early Child Development and Care*, 175(6), pp. 489–506.

Clark, A., Kjørholt, A. T. & Moss, P. (eds.) (2005) *Beyond Listening: Children's Perspectives on Early Childhood Services* (Bristol: Policy Press).

Clarke, L. (2000) *The Rise of Professional Women in France: Gender and Public Administration since 1830* (Cambridge University Press).

Claxton, G. (1990) *Teaching to Learn* (London: Cassell).

Claxton, G. (1999) 'A Mind to Learn: Education for the Age of Uncertainty'. Keynote paper to conference on *Motivation as a Condition for Learning* (University of London: Institute of Education), March.

Clerkx, L.E. & Van Ijzendoorn, M.J. (1992) 'Child Care in a Dutch Context: On the History, Current Status, and Evaluation on Non-maternal Child Care in the Netherlands' in M.E. Lamb, K. J. Sternberg, C-P. Hwang & A.G. Broberg (eds.) *Child Care in Context: Cross-Cultural Perspectives* (Hillsdale, New Jersey: Lawrence Erlbaum Associates), pp. 55–79.

Cole, M. (1996) *Cultural Psychology: A Once and Future Discipline* (Cambridge, MA: Harvard University Press).

Coninck-Smith, de N. & Gutman, M. (2004) 'Children and Youth in Public: Making Places, Learning Lessons, Claiming Territories', Introduction to special issue, *Childhood*, 11 (2), pp. 131–141.

Coolahan, J. (1981) *Irish Education: History and Structure* (Dublin: Institute of Public Administration).

Coolahan, J. (2002) *Teacher Education and the Teaching Career in an Era of Lifelong Learning* (Paris: Organisation of Economic Co-operation and Development).

Corsaro, W. (2003) 'Ethnographic Research *with* rather than *on* Preschool Children in the US and Italy', Paper presented at Trinity College Dublin on 26 May 2003.

Corsaro, W.A. (2005) *The Sociology of Childhood* (Sage: London).

Cowman, Sr M. (2007) *Growth and Development: Nurturing by Love, Language and Play* (Dublin: Daughters of Charity of St Vincent de Paul).

Cox, T. (ed.) (1996) *The National Curriculum and the Early Years* (London: Falmer Press).

Cuffaro, H.K. (1995) *Experimenting with the World: John Dewey and the Early Childhood Classroom* (NY: Teachers College Press).

Cullen, J. (2001) 'An Introduction to Understanding Learning' in V. Carpenter, H. Dixon, E. Rata and C. Rawlinson (eds.) *Theory in Practice for Educators* (NZ: Dunmore Press), pp. 47–71.

Cunningham, H. (1995) *Children and Childhood in Western Society since 1500* (London: Longman).

Curtis, A. (1997) *A Curriculum for the Preschool Years*, 2nd edition (Windsor: NFER-Wilson).

Dahlberg, G. & Moss, P. (2005) *Ethics and Politics in Early Childhood Education* (London: Routledge Falmer).

Dahlberg, G. (2005) 'Pedagogy as an Ethics of an Encounter', Keynote address at European Early Childhood Research Association Annual Conference, St Patrick's College of Education, Dublin, 1–3 September.

Dahlberg, G., Moss, P. & Pence, A. (1999) *Beyond Quality in Early Childhood Education and Care: Postmodern Perspectives* (London: Falmer Press).

Dalli, C. (2003) 'Professionalism in Early Childhood Practice: Thinking Through the Debates', Paper presented to the 13th Annual Conference of the European Early Childhood Education Research Association (EECERA), Glasgow, Scotland.

Darling, J. & Nisbet, J. (2000) 'Dewey in Britain' in J. Oelkers, & H. Rhyn (eds.) *Dewey and European Education: General Problems and Case Studies* (London: Kluwer Academic Publishers).

David, T. (1990) *Under-five – Under Educated?* (Buckingham: Open University Press).

David, T. (1993) (ed.) *Educating our Youngest Children: European Perspectives* (London: Paul Chapman Publishing).

David, T. (1996) 'Nursery Education and the National Curriculum' in T. Cox (ed.) *The National Curriculum and the Early Years* (London: Falmer Press).

David, T. (1999) (ed.) *Teaching Young Children* (London: Paul Chapman Publishing).

David, T., Goouch, K. Powell, S. & Abbott, L. (2002) Review of the literature compiled to support children in their earliest years, *Birth to Three Matters* (Research Report 444, Department for Education and Skills).

David, T., Aubrey, C., Anning, C. & Calder, P. (2003) (eds.) *British Educational Research Association Early Years Special Interest Group Review of Early Years Research* (Southwell: British Educational Research Association).

De Lissa, L. (1937) *Nursery Schools: A Foundation for the National System of Education* (London: Nursery Schools Association of Great Britain).

Department for Education and Employment (UK) (1997) *Early Years Development Partnerships and Plans* (London: HMSO).

Department of Education (1971) *Primary School Curriculum* (Dublin: The Stationery Office).

Department of Education and Science (1999a) *Ready to Learn: The White Paper on Early Childhood Education* (Dublin: The Stationery Office).

Department of Education and Science (1999b) *Revised Primary School Curriculum* (Dublin: The Stationery Office).

Department of Education and Science (UK) (1989) *A Survey of Education for Four-year-olds in Primary Classes* (London: HMSO).

Department of Education and Science (UK) (1990) *Starting with Quality: The Report of the Rumboldt Committee of Inquiry into the Quality of Educational Experiences offered to 3- and 4-year-olds* (London: HMSO).

Department of Education and Science (UK) (2007) *Statutory Framework for the Early Years Foundation Stage: Setting the Standards for Learning, Development and Care for Children from Birth to Five* (Nottingham: Department for Education and Skills).

Department of Environment, Heritage and Local Government (2001) *Childcare Facilities: Guidelines for Planning Authorities* (Dublin: The Stationery Office).

Department of Health and Children (2000) *Our Children, Their Lives: The National Children's Strategy* (Dublin: The Stationery Office).

Department of Justice, Equality and Law Reform (1999) *National Childcare Strategy* (Dublin: The Stationery Office).

Department of Justice, Equality and Law Reform (2002) *Model Framework for Education, Training and Professional Development in the Early Childhood Care and Education Sector, Developed by the Certifying Bodies Subgroup of National Childcare Co-ordinating Committee* (Dublin: Stationery Office).

Derman-Sparks, L. and the ABC Task Force (1989) *Anti-bias Curriculum: Tools for Empowering Young Children* (Washington, DC: National Association for the Education of Young Children).

Devine, D. (2002) 'Children's Citizenship and the Structuring of Adult–Child Relations in the Primary School', *Childhood*, 9, pp. 303–320.

Devine, D. (2003) *Children, Power and Schooling: How Childhood is Structured in the Primary School* (Stoke-on-Trent, UK: Trentham Books).

DeVries, R. & Kohlberg, L. (1987) *Constructivist Early Education: Overview and Comparison with other Programs* (Washington DC: NAEYC).

Dewey, J. (1902/1956) *The Child and the Curriculum* (Chicago: University of Chicago Press).

Dewey, J. (1916/1944) *Democracy and Education: An Introduction to the Philosophy of Education* (New York: Macmillan).

Dewey, J. (1938/1998) *Experience and Education* (Indiana: Kappa Delta Pi).

Dickins, M. & J. Denziloe (1998) *All Together, How to Create Inclusive Services for Disabled Children and their Families: A Practical*

Handbook for Early Years Workers (The National Early Years Network).

Dockett, S. (1999) 'Constructing Understanding through Play in the Early Years', *Journal of Early Years Education,* 6, 1, pp. 105–112.

Donaldson, M. (1978) *Children's Minds* (London: Penguin).

Douglas, F. (1994) *The History of the Irish Pre-school Playgroups Association* (Dublin: Irish Pre-school Playgroups Association).

Drummond, M.J. (1996) 'Play, Learning and the National Curriculum: Some Possibilities' in T. Cox *The National Curriculum and the Early Years* (London: Falmer Press).

Drummond, M.J. (1999) 'Another Way of Seeing' in L. Abbott and H. Moylett (eds.) *Early Education Transformed – New Millennium Series* (London: Falmer Press), pp. 48–60.

Dudek, M. (2001) *Building for Young Children: A Practical Guide to Planning, Designing and Building the Perfect Space* (London: National Early Years Network).

Dunn, J. (1987) 'Understanding Feelings: The Early Stages' in J. Bruner & H. Haste (eds.) *Making Sense: The Child's Construction of the World* (London: Methuen).

Dunn, J. (1993) *Young Children's Close Relationships: Beyond Attachment* (London: Sage).

Dunn, L. (1993) 'Proximal and Distal Features of Day Care Quality and Children's Development', *Early Childhood Research Quarterly,* 8, 2, pp. 167–192.

Dunne, J. (2005) 'Childhood and Citizenship: A Crossed Conversation', Keynote presentation at 15th Annual European Early Childhood Research Association Annual Conference, 31 August to 3 September 2005, published in *European Early Childhood Education Research Journal,* 14 (1) 2006, pp. 5–19.

Dunphy, L. (2000) 'Early Years Learning in the Primary School: A Response to the White Paper on Early Childhood Education' in Irish National Teachers Organisation (INTO)/St Patrick's College of Education (eds.) *Early Years Learning: Proceedings of Early Childhood Conference* (Dublin: INTO/St Patrick's College Publication), pp. 27–33.

Dweck, C.S. & Bempechat, J. (1980) 'Children's Theories of Intelligence: Consequences for Learning' in S.G. Paris, G.M. Olson & H. W. Stevenson (eds.) *Learning and Motivation in the Classroom* (Hillsdale, NJ: Erlbaum).

Dweck, C.S. & Leggett, E. (1988) 'A Social-cognitive Approach to Motivation and Personality', *Psychological Review*, 95, 2, pp. 256–273.

Dweck, C.S. (1999) *Self-theories: Their Role in Motivation, Personality and Development* (Philadelphia: Taylor and Francis).

Early Childhood Education Forum (1998) *Quality in Diversity in Early Learning: A Framework for Early Childhood Practitioners* (London: National Children's Bureau).

Edgeworth, M. & Edgeworth, R.L. (1798) *Practical Education*, Volume I (St Paul's Churchyard, London: J. Johnson).

Edgeworth, R.L. (1821) Letter from Richard Lovell Edgeworth to Commissioners of the Board of Education in Ireland contained in *Eighth Annual Report of the Commissioners of Education in Ireland* (P.P. 1821 (743) XI 133, National Library of Ireland).

Education Research Centre (1998) *Early Start Preschool Programme: Final Evaluation Report* (Dublin: Education Research Centre).

Edwards, C., Gandini, L. & Forman G. (eds.) (1995) *The Hundred Languages of Children: The Reggio Emilia Approach to Early Childhood Education* (NJ: Ablex Publishing Corporation).

Egan, K. (1997) *The Educated Mind: How Cognitive Tools Shape our Understanding* (London: University of Chicago Press).

Egertson, H. (2003) 'In Our Hands: The Possibility of a Better Future for our Children', Paper presented to the High/Scope conference in Dublin, Ireland.

Elkind, D. (1988) *The Hurried Child: Growing up too Fast too Soon* (Reading, MA: Addisson-Wesley).

Engle, P. (2006) 'Comprehensive Policy Implications of Child Rights' in United National Committee on the Rights of the Child, United Nations Children Fund and Bernard van Leer Foundation (eds.) *A Guide to General Comment 7: Implementing Child Rights in Early Childhood* (The Hague, Bernard van Leer Foundation), pp. 12–16.

Ennew, J. (1994) 'Time for Children or Time for Adults?' in J. Qvortrup,

M. Bardy, G. Sgritta & H. Wintersberger (eds.) *Childhood Matters: Social Theory, Practice and Politics* (Aldershot: Avebury), pp. 125–143.

NDP/CSF Evaluation Unit (2003) *Evaluation of the Equal Opportunities Childcare Programme 2000–2006* (Dublin: Government Stationery Office).

European Commission Network on Childcare (1990) *Quality in Childcare Services: Report on an EC Childcare Network*, Technical Seminar, Barcelona, 4–5 May 1990.

European Commission Network on Childcare and Other Measures (1996) *Quality Targets in Services for Young Children: Proposals for a Ten-Year Action Programme* (European Commission).

Evans, E. (1992) 'Curriculum Models and Early Childhood Education' in B. Spodek (ed.) *Handbook of Research in Early Childhood Education* (NY: The Free Press), pp. 107–134.

Factor, J. (2004) 'Tree Stumps, Manhole Covers and Rubbish Bins: The Invisible Play-lines of a Primary School Playground', *Childhood*, 11 (2), pp. 142–154.

Farrell, A., Tayler, C. & Tennent, L. (2003) 'Social Capital and Early Childhood Education' in *Perspectives on Educational Leadership*, 13 (7), pp. 1–2.

Farrell, A., Tayler, C. & Tennent, L. (2004) 'Building Social Capital in Early Childhood Education and Care: An Australian Study' in *British Education Research Journal*, 30 (5), pp. 623–635.

Fisher, J. (2002) *Starting from the Child: Teaching and Learning from 3 to 8*, 2nd edition (Buckingham: Open University Press).

Flanagan, Sr M. (2004) Personal communication with M. Kernan, November 2004.

Fog Olwig, K., & Gulløv, E. (2003) 'Towards an Anthropology of Children and Place' in K. Fog Olwig & E.Gulløv (eds.) *Children's Places* (London, Routledge), pp. 1–19.

Freeman, M.D.A. (1992) 'Beyond Conventions – Towards Empowerment' in M. Droogleever Fortuyn & M. de Langan (eds.) *Towards the Realisation of Human Rights of Children* (Amsterdam: Children's Ombudswork Foundation/Defence for Children International – Netherlands).

Freeman, M. (2000) 'The Future of Children's Rights', *Children & Society*, 14, pp. 277–293.

French, G. (2007) *Children's Early Learning and Development – A Background Paper* (Dublin: National Council for Curriculum and Assessment).

French, G. (2003) *Supporting Quality: Guidelines for Best Practice in Early Childhood Services*, 2nd edition (Dublin: Barnardos).

Furedi, F. (2001) *Paranoid Parenting: Abandon your Anxieties and be a Good Parent* (London, Allen Lane: The Penguin Press).

Gandini, L. (1998) 'Educational and Caring Spaces' in C. Edwards, L. Gandini & G. Forman *The Hundred Languages of Children: The Reggio Emilia Approach – Advanced Reflections*, 2nd edition (Greenwich, Connecticut: Ablex Publishing), pp. 161–178.

Gardner, H. (1991) *The Unschooled Mind: How Children Think and How Schools should Teach* (NY: Basic Books).

Gardner, H. (1993) *Frames of Mind: The Theory of Multiple Intelligences* (NY: Basic Books).

Gardner, H. (1995) 'Foreword: Complementary Perspectives on Reggio Emilia' in C. Edwards, L. Gandini & G. Forman (eds.) (1995) *The Hundred Languages of Children: The Reggio Emilia Approach to Early Childhood Education* (NJ: Ablex Publishing Corporation), pp. IX–XV.

Gardner, H. (1999) *The Disciplined Mind: What All Students should Understand* (NY: Simon & Schuster).

Gardner, H., Torff, B. & Hatch, T. (1996) 'The Age of Innocence Reconsidered: Preserving the Best of the Progressive Traditions in Psychology and Education' in D.R. Olson & N. Torrance (eds.) *The Handbook of Education and Human Development: New Models of Learning, Teaching and Schooling* (Oxford: Blackwell Publishers Inc).

Gaussen, T. (2002) 'Dynamic Systems Theory: Revolutionising Developmental Psychology', *Irish Journal of Psychology*, 22, 3–4, pp. 160–169.

Gibson, E.J. & Pick, A.D. (2000) *An Ecological Approach to Perceptional Learning and Development* (Oxford: Oxford University Press).

Gibson, J.J. (1979) *The Ecological Approach to Visual Perception* (Boston, Houghton Mifflin).

Gillen, J.A. & Cameron, J. A. (2003) 'A Day in the Life': Advancing a New Methodology for Cross-Cultural Research, Paper presented at the 13th Annual European Early Childhood Education Research Association Conference, University of Strathclyde, Glasgow, 3–6 September.

Glaser, R. (1984) 'Education and Thinking: The Role of Knowledge', *American Psychologist,* 39, 2, pp. 93–104.

Glassman, M. & Whaley, K. (2000) 'The Use of Long-term Projects in Early Childhood Classrooms in Light of Dewey's Educational Philosophy', *Early Childhood Research & Practice*, Vol. 2, 1, Spring Issue, pp.1–13.

Goffin, S.G. & Wilson, C. (2001) *Curriculum Models and Early Childhood Education: Appraising the Relationship,* 2nd edition (NJ: Merrill/Prentice Hall).

Goffin, S.G. (2000) *The Role of Curriculum Models in Early Childhood Education,* ERIC Document-PS-00-8.

Goldschmied, E. & Selleck, D. (1996) *Communication Between Babies in their First Year* (London: National Children's Bureau).

Goleman, D. (1996) *Emotional Intelligence: Why it can Matter More than IQ* (London: Bloomsbury).

Goncu, A. & S. Gaskins (2006) 'An Integrative Perspective on Play and Development' in A. Goncu & S. Gaskins (eds.) *Play and Development: Evolutionary, Socio-cultural and Functional Perspectives* (Mahwah, New Jersey: Lawrence Erlbaum), pp. 3–17.

Greene, S. & Hill, M. (2005) 'Researching Children's Experience: Methods and Methodological Issues' in S. Greene & D. Hogan (eds.) *Researching Children's Experience: Approaches and Methods* (London, Sage), pp. 1–21.

Greenfield, S. (2000) *The Private Life of the Brain* (London: Penguin Books).

Greenman, J. (2005) *Caring Spaces, Learning Places: Children's Environments that Work* (Bellevue, WA: Child Care Exchange Press).

Gulløv, E. (2003) 'Creating a Natural Place for Children: An

Ethnographic Study of Danish Kindergartens' in K. Fog Olwig & E. Gulløv (eds.) *Children's Places: Cross-cultural Perspectives* (London: Routledge), pp. 23–38.

Halldén, G. (2005) Contribution to symposium entitled 'Theoretical Implications of Recent Advances in Research on Everyday Life of Young Children in Modern Welfare States' at Childhoods 2005 International Conference, 29 June to 3 July 2005, Oslo, Norway. University of Oslo and Childwatch International.

Hardyment, C. (1995) Perfect Parents: *Baby-care Advice Past and Present* (Oxford: Oxford University Press).

Hare, A.J.C. (ed.) (1894) *The Life and Letters of Maria Edgeworth* (London: Edward Arnold).

Hart, R. (1979) *Children's Experience of Place* (New York: Irvington).

Hart, R. (1995) 'The Right to Play and Children's Participation' in H. Shier (ed.) *Children's Rights and Children's Play*, Article 31 action pack (Birmingham: Playtrain), pp. 21–29.

Hartley, D. (1993) *Understanding the Nursery School* (London: Cassell).

Hartman, H.J. (1998) 'Metacognition in Teaching and Learning: An Introduction', *Instructional Science*, 26, 1–2, 1–3.

Hayes, K. (2007) 'Teachers Angry at More Delays for Replacement Primary School', *The Irish Times*, 24 November 2007.

Hayes, N. & Bradley, S. (2006) 'The Childcare Question' in B. Fanning and M. Rush (eds.) *Care and Social Change in the Irish Welfare Economy* (Dublin: University College Dublin Press), pp. 163–178.

Hayes, N. (1995) *The Case for a National Policy on Early Education*, Poverty and Policy, Discussion Paper No. 2 (Dublin: Combat Poverty Agency).

Hayes, N. (1996) 'Quality in Early Childhood Education', *Irish Educational Studies,* Vol. 15, 1–13.

Hayes, N. (2001) 'Early Childhood Education in Ireland: Policy, Provision and Practice', *Administration* Vol. 49, 3, 43–67.

Hayes, N. (2002) *Children's Rights – Whose Right? A Review of Child Policy Development in Ireland*, Policy Paper (Dublin: Policy Institute, TCD).

Hayes, N. (2003) 'Play, Care and Learning: Creating an Integrated Curriculum for Early Childhood Education in Ireland' in M. Karlsson-

Lohmander I. Pramling (eds.) *Care, Play and Learning: Curricula for Early Childhood Education Volume 5, Researching Early Childhood* (Goteborg: Early Childhood Research and Development Centre/Goteborg University), pp. 69–82.

Hayes, N. (2004) 'What are Four-Year-Olds Doing at School? Reconciling Current Knowledge about Learning in Young Children with Early Educational Pedagogy', PhD Thesis (Dublin: Trinity College Dublin).

Hayes, N. (2007) *Perspectives on the Relationship between Education and Care in Early Education* (Dublin: National Council for Curriculum and Assessment).

Hayes, N. (2007) 'The Role of Early Childhood Care and Education from an Anti-poverty Perspective', Paper commissioned by the Combat Poverty Agency, Ireland, presented September 2007.

Hayes, N., O'Flaherty, J. & Kernan, M. (1997) *A Window into Early Education in Ireland: The First National Report of the IEA Pre-Primary Project* (Dublin: Dublin Institute of Technology).

Heckman, J. (2000) *Invest in the Very Young* (Chicago: Ounce of Prevention Fund).

Heerwart, E. (1906) *Fünfzig Jahre im Dienste Fröbels: Erinnerungen von Eleonare Heerwart* [Fifty Years in the Service of Froebel: Memories of Eleonare Heerwart] (Eisenach: H. Kahle).

Heft, H. (1988) 'Affordances of Children's Environments: A Functional Approach to Environmental Description', *Children's Environments Quarterly*, 5, 29–37.

Heiland, H. (1993) Friedrich Fröbel (1782–1852) in *PROSPECTS*: the quarterly review of comparative education, Vol. XXIII, (3/4), 473–91.

Hendricks, B. (2001) *Designing for Play* (Aldershot, Ashgate).

Herrenstein, R.J. & Murray, C. (1994) *The Bell Curve: Intelligence and Class Structure in American Life* (NY: Simon Schuster).

Heyman, G.D., Dweck, C.S. & Cain, K.M. (1992) 'Young Children's Vulnerability to Self-blame and Helplessness: Relationship to Beliefs about Goodness', *Child Development*, 63, 401–415.

High/Scope Educational Research Foundation (2003) High/Scope's Approach for Toddlers in Group Care: Arranging and Equipping the

Environment, participant guide (field-test edition) (Ypsilanti, Michigan: The High/Scope Educational Research Foundation).

Hilgard, E.R. (1996) 'History of Educational Psychology' in D.C. Berliner & R.C. Calfee (eds.) *Handbook of Educational Psychology* (London: Simon & Schuster Macmillan), pp. 990–1004.

Hillman, M.J., Adams, J. & Whitelegg, J. (1990) *One False Move: A Study of Children's Independent Mobility* (London: Policy Studies Institute).

Hirst, K. (2001) 'A Journey into Reality' in L. Abbott & C. Nutbrown, (eds.) *Experiencing Reggio Emilia: Implications for Preschool Provision* (Buckingham: Open University Press), pp. 106–112.

Hogan, D. (2005) 'Researching "the child" in Developmental Psychology' in S. Greene & D. Hogan (eds.) *Researching Children's Experiences* (London: Sage), pp. 22–41.

Hohmann, M. & Weikart, D. (1995) *Educating Young Children: Active Learning Practices for Preschool and Childcare Programs* (Ypsilanti, MI: HighScope Press).

Hohmann, M. & Weikart, D.P. (2002) *Educating Young Children: Active Practices for Preschool and Child Care Programs* (Ypsilanti, Michigan, High/Scope Press).

Holland, S. (1979) *Rutland Street: The Story of an Educational Experiment for Disadvantaged Children in Dublin* (Oxford, Pergamon Press and The Hague, the Bernard Van Leer Foundation).

Holloway, S.L. & Valentine, G. (2000) 'Children's Geographies and the New Social Order' in S.L. Holloway & G. Valentine (eds.) *Children's Geographies: Playing, Living and Learning* (London: Routledge), pp. 1–28.

Hoof, D. (1977) *Handbuch der spieltheorie Fröbel's Untersuchungen und Materialienzum Vorschulischen Lernen* [Manual of Froebel's Play Theory, Investigations and Materials for Pre-school Teaching and Learning] (Braunschweig: Westermann.

Horgan, M. (1995) 'Early Years Education in Ireland – A Case Study of One Junior Infant Class', *Education Today*, Vol. 3, 3, pp. 6–9.

Hutt, S.J., Tyler, C., Hutt, C. & Chrisopherson, H. (1989) *Play, Exploration and Learning* (London: Routledge).

Ireland (1998) *Report of the Forum of Early Childhood Education* (Dublin: Government Stationery Office).

Ireland (1999a) *Ready to Learn: White Paper on Early Childhood Education* (Dublin: Government Stationery Office).

Ireland (1999b) *The Primary School Curriculum* (Dublin: Government Stationery Office).

Ireland (2000) *Our Children – Our Lives: The National Children's Strategy* (Dublin: Government Stationery Office).

Ireland (2002) *Model Framework for Education, Training and Professional Development in the Early Childhood Sector* (Dublin: Government Stationery Office).

Irish Builder, The (1890) *Notes of Works in The Irish Builder*, 15 April 1890.

Irish National Teachers Organisation (1995) *Early Childhood Education* (Dublin: INTO).

James, A. & James, A. (2004) *Constructing Childhood: Theory, Policy and Social Practice* (Basingstoke: Palgrave Macmillan).

James, A. (2001) 'Ethnography in the Study of Children and Childhood' in P. Atkinson, A. Coffey, S. Delamont, J. Lofland & L. Lofland *Handbook of Ethnography* (London: Sage Publications), pp. 246–257.

James, A., Jenks, C., & Prout, A. (1998) *Theorizing Childhood* (Cambridge: Polity).

Johnson, J. E. (1988) 'Psychological Theory and Early Education' in A. D. Pellegrini (ed.) *Psychological Bases for Early Education* (New York: John Wiley & Sons), pp. 1–22.

Johnston, M. (1985) *Around the Banks of Pimlico* (Dublin: Attic Press).

Kahn, P. H., Jr (2005) 'Encountering the Other: Children, Youth and Environments', 15(2), 392–397. Retrieved January 2006 from http://www.colorado.edu/journals/cye/.

Kamin, M. L. & Dweck, C.S. (1999) 'Person versus Process Praise and Criticism: Implications for Contingent Self-worth and Coping', *Developmental Psychology*, 35, 835–847.

Karmiloff–Smith, A. (1992) *Beyond Modularity: A Developmental Perspective on Cognitive Science* (Cambridge MA: Cambridge University Press).

Karsten, L. (2002) 'Mapping Childhood in Amsterdam: The Spatial and Social Construction of Children's Domains in the City', *Tijdschrift voor Economische en Sociale Geografie*, 93, pp. 231–241.

Katz, L. (1993) *Dispositions: Definitions and Implications for Early Childhood Practices.* Perspectives from ERIC/ECCE: a monograph series (Urbana, Illinois: ERIC Clearinghouse on ECCE).

Katz, L. & Chard, S.C. (1994) *Engaging Children's Minds: The Project Approach,* 2nd edition (Norwood, NJ: Ablex Publishing).

Katz, L. (1985) 'Dispositions in Early Childhood Education', *ERIC/EECE Bulletin,* 18, 2, 1–3.

Katz, L. (1988) 'What Should Young Children be Doing?' *American Educator,* Summer, pp. 29–45.

Katz, L. (1995) 'What Can we Learn from Reggio Emilia?' in C. Edwards, L. Gandini, G. Forman (eds.) *The Hundred Languages of Children: The Reggio Emilia Approach to Early Childhood Education* (NJ: Ablex Publishing Corporation), pp. 19–37.

Katz, L. (1996) 'Child Development Knowledge and Teacher Preparation: Confronting Assumptions', *Early Childhood Research Quarterly* 11, p. 135–146.

Kellaghan, T. (1977) *The Evaluation of an Intervention Programme for Disadvantaged Children* (Windsor, Berks: NFER Publishing).

Kellaghan, T. & Greaney, B.J. (1993) *The Educational Development of Students Following Participation in a Preschool Programme in a Disadvantaged Area* (Dublin: Educational Research Centre).

Kernan, M. (1989) 'An Exploratory Study of the Beliefs and Behaviour of a Sample of Reception Class Teachers: London and Dublin Compared', Unpublished MA Thesis, Institute of Education, University of London.

Kernan, M. (2005) 'Developing Citizenship through Supervised Play: The Civics Institute of Ireland Playgrounds, 1933–75', *History of Education*, 34(6), 675–687.

Kernan, M. (2006) 'The Place of the Outdoors in Constructions of a "Good" Childhood: An Interdisciplinary Study of Outdoor Provision in Early Childhood Education in Urban Settings', Unpublished PhD Thesis, University College Dublin.

Kernan, M. (2007) 'Play as a Context for Early Learning and Development', Background paper for the *National Framework for Early Learning* (Dublin: National Council for Curriculum and Assessment).

Kirkby, M. (1989) 'Nature as Refuge in Children's Environments', *Children's Environments Quarterly*, 6, 7–12.

Kjørholt, A.T. & Tingstad, V. (2007) 'Flexible Places – Flexible Children? Discourses on Freedom and Autonomy Inscribed in New Design of the Kindergarten' in H. Zeiher, D. Devine, A. Kjørholt & H. Strandell (eds.) *Children's Times and Spaces: Changes in Welfare in an Intergenerational Perspective* (Odense: University Press of Southern Denmark).

Kjørholt, A.T., Moss, P. & Clark, A. (2005) 'Beyond Listening: Future Prospects' in A. Clark, P. Moss & A.T. Kjørholt (eds) *Beyond Listening: Children's Perspectives on Early Childhood Services* (Bristol: Policy Press), pp. 175–187.

Krappmann, L. (2006) 'The Right of the Young Child to Rest, Leisure and Play' in United Nations Committee on the Rights of the Child, United Nations Children Fund and Bernard van Leer Foundation (2006) *A Guide to General Comment 7: Implementing Child Rights in Early Childhood* (The Hague: Bernard van Leer Foundation), pp. 81–82.

Kuhn, D. (1992) 'Cognitive Development' in M.H. Bornstein & M.E. Lamb (eds.) *Developmental Psychology: An Advanced Textbook*, 3rd edition (Hillsdale, NJ: Lawrence Erlbaum Associates), pp. 211–272.

Kuhn, D. (1995) 'Microgenetic Study of Change: What Has it Told Us?', *Psychological Science*, 6, pp. 133–139.

Kuhn, D. (1997) 'The View from Giants' Shoulders' in L. Smith, J. Dockrell & P. Tomlinson (eds.) *Piaget, Vygotsky and Beyond: Future Issues for Developmental Psychology and Education* (London: Routledge), pp. 246–259.

Kuhn, D. (1999) 'Metacognitive Development' in L. Balter & C.S. Tamis-LeMonda (eds.) *Child Psychology: A Handbook of Contemporary Issues* (NY: Taylor and Francis Group), pp. 259–286.

Kytta, M. (2002) 'Affordances of Children's Environments in the Context of Cities, Small Towns, Suburbs and Rural Villages in Finland and

Belarus', *Journal of Environmental Psychology*, 22, pp. 109–123.

Kytta, M. (2004) 'The Extent of Children's Independent Mobility and the Number of Actualised Affordances as Criteria for Child-friendly Environments', *Journal of Environmental Psychology*, 24, pp. 179–198.

Laevers, F. (1994) *The Innovative Project Experiential Education* (Leuwen: Research Centre for Early Childhood and Primary Education).

Laevers, F. (2002) (ed.) *Research on Experiential Education: A Selection of Articles* (Leuwen: Centre for Experiential Education).

Lamb, M.E. & Hwang, C.P. (1996) 'Images of Childhood: An Introduction' in C.P. Hwang, M.E. Lamb, & I.E. Sigel (eds.) *Images of Childhood* (New Jersey: Lawrence Erlbaum Associates), pp. 1–12.

Lamb, M.E., Sternberg, K.J., Hwang, C. P. & Broberg, A.G. (eds.) (1992) *Child Care in Context: Cross-Cultural Perspectives* (Hillsdale, New Jersey: Lawrence Erlbaum Associates).

Lambert, E.B. and Clyde, M. (2000) *Rethinking Early Childhood Theory and Practice* (Australia: Social Science Press).

Lansdown, G. (1994) 'Children's Rights' in B. Mayall (ed.) *Children's Childhoods: Observed and Experienced* (London: Falmer Press), pp. 33–44.

Lareau, A. (2003) *Unequal Childhoods: Class, Race and Family Life* (Berkeley, University of California Press).

Larkin, S. (2002) 'Creating Metacognitive Experiences for 5- and 6-year-old Children' in M. Shayer & P. Adey (eds) *Learning Intelligence – Cognitive Acceleration across the Curriculum from 5 to 15 Years.* (Buckingham: Open University Press), pp. 65–79.

Lave, J. & Wenger, E. (1991) *Situated Learning: Legitimate Peripheral Participation* (Cambridge: Cambridge University Press).

Leseman, P., Rollenberg, L. & Rispens, J. (2001) 'Playing and Working in Kindergarten: Cognitive Co-construction in Two Educational Situations', *Early Childhood Research Quarterly*, Vol. 16, (3) pp. 363–384.

Liebschner, J. (1991) *Foundations of Progressive Education: The History of the National Froebel Society* (Cambridge: Lutterworth Press).

Liebschner, J. (1992) *A Child's Work: Freedom and Play in Froebel's Educational Theory and Practice* (Cambridge: Lutterworth Press).

Lilley, I. M. (1967) *Friedrich Froebel: A Selection from his Writings* (London: Cambridge University Press).

Lindon, J. (2001) *Understanding Children's Play* (Cheltenham, Nelson Thornes).

Locke, J. (1963) *Some Thoughts Concerning Education* (Yolton & Yolton, 2000).

Louv, R. (2005) *Last Child in the Woods: Saving our Children from Nature-deficit Disorder* (Chapel Hill, Nth Carolina: Algonquin).

Lubeck, S. (1996) 'Deconstructing Child Development: Knowledge and Teacher Preparation', *Early Childhood Research Quarterly*, 21, pp. 147–167.

Luddy, M. (1995) *Women and Philanthropy in Nineteenth-century Ireland* (Cambridge: Cambridge University Press).

Luddy, M. (1998) 'Religion, Philanthropy and the State in Late Eighteenth- and Early Nineteenth-century Ireland' in H. Cunningham & J. Innes (eds.) *Charity, Philanthropy and Reform* (London: Macmillan), pp. 148–167.

Lyons, C.W. (2002) 'Conceptions of Intelligence and Educational Disadvantage', *Irish Educational Studies*, Vol. 21, No. 1, p. 18.

McCann, P. & Young, F.A. (1982) *Samuel Wilderspin and the Infant School Movement* (Beckenham: Croom Helm).

McFarlane, K. & Lewis, T. (2004) 'Childcare — Human Service or Education: A Genealogical Approach', *Contemporary Issues in Early Childhood*, Vol. 5, No. 1, pp. 51–67.

McGough, A. (2002) 'Addressing Disadvantage: The Role of Teaching in Primary Education' in *Primary Education: Ending Disadvantage: Proceedings and Action Plan of National Forum* (Dublin: St Patrick's College, Drumcondra), pp. 73–85.

McKendrick, J.H. (2000) 'The Geography of Children: An Annotated Bibliography', *Childhood*, 7(3), pp. 359–387.

McMillan, M. (1920) *Nursery Schools: A Practical Handbook* (London).

McMillan, M. (1930) *The Nursery School* (London: J.M. Dent & Sons).

McMillan, M. (n.d.) *Nursery Schools and the Pre-school Child*, Booklet accessed in the records of the Civics Institute of Ireland, Dublin City Archives, Pearse Street, Dublin.

McNaughton, G. (2005) *Doing Foucault in Early Childhood Studies: Applying Post-structural Ideas* (London: Routledge & Falmer Press).

McNaughton, G. (2000) *Rethinking Gender in Early Childhood Education* (Sydney: Allen & Unwin).

McNaughton, G. (2003) *Shaping Early Childhood: Learners, Curriculum and Contexts* (Maidenhead: Open University Press).

Mallaguzzi, I. (1993) 'For an Education Based on Relationships', *Young Children*, 49, pp. 9–12.

Manning-Morton, J. & Thorp, M. (2003) *Key Times for Play: The First Three Years* (Maidenhead, Berkshire: Open University Press).

Marcon, R. A. (1999) 'Differential Impact of Preschool Models on Development and Early Learning of Inner-city Children: A Three Cohort Study', *Developmental Psychology*, 35, 2, pp. 358–375.

Margolis, E. & Fram, S. (2007) 'Caught Napping: Images of Surveillance, Discipline and Punishment on the Body of the Schoolchild' in *History of Education*, 36, 2, pp. 191–211.

Mayall, B. (2002) *Towards a Sociology for Childhood* (Buckingham: Open University Press).

Meadows, S. (1993) *The Child as Thinker* (NY: Routledge).

Miller, J. (1997) *Never Too Young: How Young Children Can Take Responsibility and Make Decisions: A Handbook for Early Years Workers* (London: National Early Years Network).

Ministry of Children and Family Affairs (1996) *Framework Plan for Day Care Institutions – a brief presentation* (Oslo: Norwegian Ministry of Children and Family Affairs).

Ministry of Children and Family Affairs (2001) *OECD – Thematic Review of Early Childhood Education and Care Policy in Norway: Background Paper* (Oslo: Norwegian Ministry of Children and Family Affairs).

Montessori, M. (1964) *The Montessori Method* (Cambridge MA: Robert Bentley), retrieved October 2003 from http://www.itl.

Montgomery, D.H. (n.d.) *Life in a Junior School: The Growth, Experiences and Development, Physical, Intellectual and Emotional, of Children between the Ages of Four and Twelve Years* (Dublin: Rathgar Junior School).

Moorcock, K. (1998) *Swings and Roundabouts: The Danger of Safety in Outdoor Play Environments* (Sheffield Hallam University).

Moore, G.T. (1985) 'State of the Art in Play Environment' in J.L. Frost & S. Sunderlin (eds.) *When Children Play*, Wheaton MD, Association for Childhood Education International, pp. 171–189.

Moore, R.C. (1986) *Childhood's Domain: Play and Place in Child Development* (London: Croom Helm).

Morgan, M. (2002) 'Too Much Knowledge, Too Much Fear: Curricular Developments in Irish Primary Schools' in J. Dunne and J. Kelly (eds.) *Childhood and its Discontents: The First Seamus Heaney Lectures* (Dublin: Liffey Press), pp. 107–122.

Moss, P. & Petrie, P. (2002) *From Children's Services to Children's Spaces* (London: Routledge Falmer).

Moss, P. (2001) 'The Otherness of Reggio' in L. Abbott & C. Nutbrown (eds.) (2001) *Experiencing Reggio Emilia: Implications for Preschool Provision* (Buckingham: Open University Press), pp. 125–137.

Moss, P. (2005) 'Making the Narrative of Quality Stutter', *Early Education and Development*, 16(4), pp. 406–420.

Moss, P. (2007) 'Bring Politics into the Nursery: Early Childhood Education as a Democratic Practice', Working papers in Early Childhood Development, No. 43. (The Hague: Bernard van Leer Foundation).

Moyles, J. (1988) *Just Playing: The Role and Status of Play in Early Childhood Education* (Milton Keynes: Open University Press).

Moyles, J. (ed.) (1994) *The Excellence of Play* (Buckingham: Open University Press).

Murphy, B. (2004) 'Irish Senior Infant Classroom Practice – A Case for Imaginary Play?', Paper presented to the OMEP (Ireland) Annual Conference, Dublin, 24 April.

Murray, C. & O'Doherty, A. (2001) *Éist: Respecting Diversity in Early Childhood Care, Education and Training* (Dublin: Pavee Point).

Nabhan, G.P. & Trimble, S. (1994) *The Geography of Childhood: Why Children Need Wild Places* (Boston: Beacon Press).

National Children's Nurseries Association (2002) *We Like this Place: Guidelines for Best Practice in the Design of Childcare Facilities* (Dublin: National Children's Nurseries Association).

National Children's Office (2004) *Ready, Steady, Play! A National Play Policy* (Dublin: Stationery Office).

National Council for Curriculum and Assessment (2004) *Towards a Framework for Early Learning: Consultative Document* (Dublin: NCCA).

National Council for Curriculum and Assessment (2005) *Towards a Framework for Early Learning: Final Consultative Report* (Dublin: NCCA).

National Council for Curriculum and Assessment (forthcoming) *The Framework for Early Learning* (Dublin: NCCA).

National Economic and Social Forum (NESF) (2005) *Early Childhood Care and Education*, Forum Report No. 31 (Dublin: National Economic and Social Forum).

New Zealand (1996) *Te Whariki: Early Childhood Curriculum* (Wellington, NZ: Learning Media Ltd).

New, R.S., Mardell, B. & Robinson, D. (2005) 'Early Childhood Education as Risky Business: Going Beyond what's "Safe" to Discovering What's Possible, *Early Childhood Research & Practice* (7), 2, retrieved July 2006 http://ecrp.uiuc.edu/v7n2/new.html.

Newson, J. & Newson, E. (1976) *Seven Years Old in the Home Environment* (London: Allen & Unwin).

Nieuwenhuys, O. (2003) 'Places of Children and the Non-place of Childhood in Poomkara' in K. Fog Olwig and E. Gullöv (eds.) *Children's Places* (London, Routledge), pp. 99–118.

Nutbrown, C. (1996) *Respectful Educators, Capable Learners: Young Children's Rights and Early Education* (Taylor & Francis).

O'Connor, A. & Parkes, S. (1983) *Gladly Learn, Gladly Teach: A History of Alexandra College and School, Dublin 1866–1916* (Dublin: Blackwater Press).

O'Dwyer, F. (1992) 'Tyrone House and the Department of Education', Unpublished report for Department of Education, dated 15 November 1992.

O'Sullivan, E. (2001) '"Mercy unto thousands" – Constructing the Institutional Child' in A. Cleary, M. Nic Giolla Phadraig & S. Quinn (eds.) *Understanding Children, Volume 1: State, Education and Economy* (Cork, Oak Tree Press), pp. 45–78.

OECD (2000) *Starting Strong: Early Childhood Education and Care* (Paris: Organisation for Economic Co-operation and Development).

OECD (2002) 'Strengthening Early Childhood Programmes: A Policy Framework' in *Education Policy Analysis* (Paris: Organisation for Economic Co-operation and Development), pp. 9–33.

OECD (2004), OECD thematic review of early childhood education and care policy in Ireland: country note for Ireland (Dublin: The Stationery Office).

OECD (2006) *Starting Strong II: Early Childhood Education and Care* (Paris: Organisation for Economic Co-operation and Development).

Olds, A. (1988) 'Designing for Play: Beautiful Spaces are Playful Places', *Children's Health Care*, 16(3), pp. 218–222.

OMNA (2000) *The Final Report of the OMN–DIT/NOW Early Childhood Project 1995–2000* (Dublin: DIT).

Owen, R. ([1813] 1970) 'A New View of Society' in V.A.C. Gatrell (ed.) *Report to the County of Lanark, A New View of Society* (Middlesex, England: Pelican), pp. 87–198.

Owen, R. (1824) *An Outline of the System of Education at New Lanark* (Glasgow).

Packer, M.J. (1993) 'Away from Internalisation' in E.A. Forman, N. Minick & C.A. Stone (eds.) *Contexts for Learning: Sociocultural Dynamics in Children's Development* (NY: Oxford University Press), pp. 254–265.

Paley, V. Gussin (1992) *You Can't Say You Can't Play* (Cambridge, MA: Harvard University Press).

Parker-Rees, R. (1999) 'Play and the Disposition of Playfulness' in L. Abbott & H. Moylett (eds.) *Early Education Transformed* (London: Falmer press), pp. 61–72.

Pascal, C. & Bertram, T. (1993) 'The Education of Young Children and their Teachers in Europe', *European Early Childhood Education Research Journal*, Vol. 1, No. 2, pp. 27–38.

Pellegrini, A. D. & Bjorklund, D.F. (1998) *Applied Child Study: A Developmental Approach*, 2nd edition (Hillsdale, NJ: Lawrence Erlbaum Associates).

Pellegrini, A.D. & Blatchford, P. (2000) *Children's Interactions at School: Peers and Teachers* (London: Edward Arnold).

Pellegrini, A.D. & Smith, P.K. (1998) 'Physical Activity Play: The Nature and Function of a Neglected Aspect of Play', *Child Development*, 69, 1, pp. 577–598.

Peller, L. (1996) 'The Children's House', *The NAMTA Journal*, 21, 3, pp. 9–23.

Penn, H. (1997) *Comparing Nurseries: Staff and Children in Italy, Spain and the UK* (London: Paul Chapman).

Penn, H. (2000) (ed.) *Early Childhood Services, Theory, Policy and Practice* (Buckingham: Open University Press).

Penn, H. (2001) 'Culture and Childhood in Pastoralist Communities: The Example of Outer Mongolia' in L. Alanen and B. Mayall (eds.) *Conceptualizing Adult–Child Relationships* (London: Falmer Press), pp. 86–98.

Perkins, D. N., Jay, E. & Tishman, S. (1993) 'Beyond Abilities: A Dispositional Theory of Thinking' in *Merrill-Palmer Quarterly*, Vol. 39, No. 1, pp. 1–21.

Petrie, P. (2004) 'Extending Pedagogy', *Journal of Education and Training*, Vol. 31, No.4, pp. 193 – 196.

Piaget, J. (1971) 'The Theory of Stages in Cognitive Development' in D.R. Green, M.P. Ford & G.B. Flanner (eds.) *Measurement and Piaget* (NY: McGraw-Hill).

Pianta, R.C., Howes, C., Burchinal, M., Bryant, D., Clifford, R., Early, D. and Barbarin, O. (2005) 'Features of Pre-kindergarten Programmes, Classrooms and Teachers. Do They Predict Observed Quality and Child-teacher Interactions?', *Applied Developmental Sciences*, 9(3), pp. 144–159.

Pinker, S. (2002) *The Blank Slate* (London: Penguin Books).

Pramling Samuelsson, I. (2003) 'How Do Children Tell Their Childhood?', Keynote address at 13th Annual European Early Childhood Education Research Conference, University of Strathclyde,

Glasgow, Scotland, 3–6 September.

Preston, M. (1996) 'Women and Philanthropy in Nineteenth-century Dublin', *The Historian*, 58, pp. 763–776.

Prunty, J. (1999) *Dublin Slums 1800–1925: A Study in Urban Geography* (Dublin: Academic Press).

Pugh, G. (1996) *Contemporary Issues in the Early Years* (London: National Children's Bureau).

QCA (1999) *Early Learning Goals* (London: Qualification and Curriculum Authority).

QCA (2001) *Curriculum Guidance for the Foundation Stage* (London: Qualification and Curriculum Authority).

QCA/DfEE (2000) *Curriculum Guidance for the Foundation Stage* (London: Qualification and Curriculum Authority).

Qvortrup, J. (1995) 'Childhood Matters: An Introduction' in J. Qvortrup, M. Bardy, G. Sgritta, & H. Wintersberger (eds.) *Childhood Matters: Social Theory, Practice and Politics* (Aldershot, Avebury), pp. 1–24.

Ramey, C., Campbell, F., Burchinal, M., Skinner, M., Gardner, D. & Ramey, S. (2000) 'Persistent Effects of Early Childhood Education on High-risk Children and their Mothers', *Applied Developmental Science*, Vol. 4, No. 1, pp. 2–14.

Ramey, C.T. & Ramey, S.L. (1998) 'Early Intervention and Early Experience', *American Psychologist*, 53 (2), pp. 109–120.

Reed, E.S. (1996) *Encountering the World: Toward an Ecological Psychology* (Oxford: Oxford University Press).

Report of Commission on the Family (1998) *Strengthening Families for Life*, Final Report of the Commission on the Family to the Minister for Social Community and Family Affairs (Dublin: Stationery Office).

Resnick, L. & Nelson-Le Gall, S. (1997) 'Socializing Intelligence' in L. Smith, J. Dockrell & P. Tomlinson (eds.) (1997) *Piaget, Vygotsky and Beyond: Future Issues for Developmental Psychology and Education* (London: Routledge), pp. 145–158.

Resnick, L.B. & Klopfer, L.E. (1989) 'Towards a Thinking Curriculum: An Overview' in L.B. Resnick & L.E. Klopfer (eds.) *Towards a Thinking Curriculum: Current Cognitive Research* (Alex, VA: American Society for Curriculum and Development).

Resnick, L.B. (1987) 'Learning in and out of School', *Educational Research*, 16, pp. 13–20.

Rinaldi, C. (1995) 'The Emergent Curriculum and Social Constructivism', an interview with Lella Gandini in C. Edwards, L. Gandini, & G. Forman (eds.) *The Hundred Languages of Children: The Reggio Emilia Approach to Early Childhood Education* (NJ: Ablex Publishing Corporation), pp. 101–111.

Rinaldi, C. (1998) 'The Space of Childhood' in G. Ceppi & M. Zini (eds.) *Children, Spaces, Relations: Metaproject for an Environment for Young Children* (Reggio Emilia:Reggio Children and Comune di Reggio Emilia), pp. 114–120.

Rivkin, M. (1995) *The Great Outdoors: Restoring Children's Right to Play Outdoors* (Washington DC: National Association for the Education of Young Children).

Rodgers, S. (1999) *Planning an Appropriate Curriculum for the Under Fives* (London: David Fulton Publishers).

Rogoff (1997) 'Evaluating Development in the Process of Participation: Theory, Methods and Practice Building on Each Other' in E. Amsel & K.A. Renninger (eds.) *Change and Development: Issues of Theory, Method and Application* (NJ: Lawerence Ehrlbaum Associates), pp. 265–285.

Rogoff, B. (1990) *Apprenticeship in Thinking: Cognitive Development in Social Context* (NY: Oxford University Press).

Rogoff, B., Correa-Chávez M. & Navichoc Cotuc, M. (2005) 'Schooling in Human Development' in D.B. Pillemer & S.H. White (eds.) *Developmental Psychology and Social Change: Research, History and Policy* (New York: Cambridge University Press), pp. 225–263.

Rogoff, B. (1998) 'Cognition as a Collaborative Process' in W. Damon, D. Kuhn and R.S. Siegler (eds.) *Handbook of Child Psychology (Vol. 2): Cognition, Language and Perceptual Development* (New York: Wiley), pp. 679–744.

Rogoff, B. (2003) *The Cultural Nature of Human Development* (Oxford: Oxford University Press).

Rogoff, B., Mosier, C., Mistry, J. & Goncu, A. (1993) 'Toddlers Guided Participation with their Caregivers in Cultural Activity' in E.A.

Forman, N. Minick & C.A. Stone (eds.) *Contexts for Learning* (NY: Oxford University Press).

Roopnarine, J.L. & Johnson, J.E. (eds.) (2000) *Approaches to Early Childhood Education*, 3rd edition (London: Merrill).

Rousseau J.J. (1762) *Émile*, English translation retrieved October 2003 from http://www.itl.columbia.edu/pedagogies/rousseau.

Rubin, K.H., Fein, G.G. & Vandenberg, B. (1983) 'Play' in P.H. Mussen & E.M. Hetherington (eds.) *Handbook of Child Psychology, Vol. IV: Socialisation, Personality and Social Development* (New York: John Wiley), pp. 693–774.

Rutter, M. (1985) 'Family and School Influences on Cognitive Development', *Journal of Child Psychology*, 26, 5, pp. 683–704.

Ryan, A. (1995) *John Dewey and the High Tide of American Liberalism* (NY: Norton and Co.).

Sayeed, Z. & Guerin, E. (2000) *Early Years Play: A Happy Medium for Assessment and Intervention* (London: David Fulton Publishers), pp. 32–34.

Schon, D. (1983) *The Reflective Practitioner. How Professionals Think in Action* (NY: Basic Books).

Schweinhart, L. & Weikart, D. (1997) *Lasting Differences: The High/Scope Preschool Curriculum Comparison through age 23*, Monograph 12 (Ypsilanti, MI: HighScope Press), pp. 83–94.

Schweinhart, L., Barnes, H. and Weikart, D. (1993) *Significant Benefits: The High/Scope Perry Preschool Study through age 27* (Ypsilanti, MI: HighScope Press).

Scottish Consultative Council on the Curriculum (1999) *A Curriculum Framework for Children 3 to 5* (Dundee: SCCC).

Shayer, M. & Adey, P. (eds.) (2002) *Learning Intelligence: Cognitive Acceleration across the Curriculum from 5 to 15 years* (Buckingham: Open University Press).

Shepard, P. (1969) 'Ecology and Man – A Viewpoint', introduction in P. Shepard & D. McKinley (eds.) *The Subversive Science: Essays Toward an Ecology of Man* (Boston: Houghton Mifflin Company), pp. 1–10.

Shonkoff, J.P. & Phillips, D.A. (2002) *From Neurons to*

Neighbourhoods: The Science of Early Childhood Development (Washington DC: National Academy Press).

Shore, R. (1997) *Rethinking the Brain: New Insights into Early Development* (NY: Family and Work Institute).

Sidy, V. (2003) 'Buildings that Nurture' in *The Namta Journal*, 28, 2, pp. 143–154.

Siegler, R.S. (1996) *Emerging Minds: The Process of Change in Children's Thinking* (Oxford: Oxford University Press).

Sigel, I.E. (1996) 'Disciplinary Approaches to Images of Childhood: Religion, History, Anthropology and Psychology' in C.P. Hwang, M.E. Lamb, I.E. Sigel (eds.) *Images of Childhood* (Mahwah, New Jersey: Lawrence Erlbaum Associates), pp. 12–74.

Singer, E. & de Haan, D. (2007) *The Social Lives of Young Children: Play, Conflict and Moral Learning in Day-care Groups* (Amsterdam: BV Uitgeverij SWP).

Siraj-Blatchford, I. (2003) Keynote Address to the Annual Meeting of the Irish Preschool Playgroups Association, September.

Siraj-Blatchford, I. (2004) 'Quality Teaching in the Early Years' in A. Anning, J. Cullen & M. Fleer (eds.) *Early Childhood Education: Society and Culture* (London: Sage Publications), pp. 137–148.

Smidt, S. (2006) *The Developing Child in the 21st Century: A Global Perspective on Child Development* (London: Routledge).

Smiley, P. A. & Dweck, C.S. (1994) 'Individual Differences in Achievement Goals Among Young Children', *Child Development* 65, pp. 1723–1743.

Smith, P.K. (1986) *Children's Play: Research, Development and Practical Application* (NY: Gordon & Breach).

Smith, S.J. (1998) *Risk and our Pedagogical Relation to Children: On the Playground and Beyond* (Albany: State University New York Press).

Standing, E.M. (1957) *Maria Montessori: Her Life and Work* (London: Hollis & Carter).

Steedman, C. (1990) *Childhood, Culture and Class in Britain: Margaret McMillan 1860–1931* (London: Virago Press).

Stein, S. (2001) *Noah's Children: Restoring the Ecology of Childhood* (New York: North Point Press).

Stephenson, A. (2003) 'Physical Risk-taking: Dangerous or Endangered', *Early Years*, 23 (1), pp. 35–43.

Sternberg, R. (1998) *Beyond IQ: A Triarchic Theory of Human Intelligence* (NY: Cambridge University Press).

Stoll Lillard, A. (2005) *Montessori: The Science behind the Genius* (Oxford: Oxford University Press).

Sumsion, J. (2006) 'The Corporatization of Australian Childcare: Towards an Ethical Audit and Research Agenda', *Journal of Childhood Research*, 4 (2), pp. 99–120.

Sutton-Smith, B. (1997) *The Ambiguity of Play* (Cambridge, Mass: Harvard University Press).

Sylva, K. (1994a) 'The Impact of Early Learning on Children's Later Development' in C. Ball *Start Right: The Importance of Early Learning* (London: RSA), pp. 84–96.

Sylva, K. (1994b) 'School Influences on Children's Development', *Journal of Child Psychology and Psychiatry*, 34, 1, pp. 135–170.

Sylva, K. (1997) 'Psychological Theory that "Works" in the Classroom' in L. Smith, J. Dockrell & P. Tomlinson (eds.) *Piaget, Vygotsky and Beyond: Future Issues for Developmental Psychology and Education* (London: Routledge).

Sylva, K., Melhuish, E., Sammons, P., Siraj-Blatchford, I. & Taggart, B. (2004) *The Effective Provision of Pre-School Education (EPPE) Project: Final Report* (London: Institute of Education/Surestart).

Sylva, K., Roy, C. & Painter, M. (1980) *Childwatching at Playgroup and Nursery School* (London: Grant McIntyre).

Sylva, K., Siraj-Blatchford, I. & Johnson, S. (1992) 'The Impact of the UK National Curriculum on Preschool Practice: Some 'Top-down' Processes at Work', *International Journal of Early Childhood*, Vol. 24, pp. 40–53.

Tanner, L.N. (1997) *Dewey's Laboratory School: Lessons for Today* (NY: Teachers College Press).

Tarpey, Sr Simeon (1963) 'Modern Teaching Methods' in the *Irish Nurse*, pp. 125–130.

Tavecchio, L. (2005) Kinderopvang: 'Opvoedingsmilieu Tussen Gezin en School' [educational practice between family and school] in M.H.

Ijzendoorn & H. de Frankrijker (eds.) *Pedagogiek in Beeld: een Inleiding in de Pedagogische Studie van Opvoeding, Onderiwijs en Hulperlening* [current pedagogical issues in the pedagogical study of child-rearing, education and interventions], 2nd edition (Houten, Bohn Stafleu van Loghum), pp. 127–141.

Taylor Allen, A. (2000) 'Children Between Public and Private worlds: The Kindergarten and Public Policy in Germany, 1840 – present' in R. Wollons (ed.) *Kindergarten & Cultures* (New Haven: Yale University Press), pp. 16–41.

Thomas, G. & Hocking, G. (2003) 'Other People's Children', Demos, retrieved September 2005 from www.demos.co.uk.

Tizard, B. & Hughes, M. (1984) *Young Children Learning* (London: Fontana).

Tobin, J.J., Wu, D.Y.H. & Davidson, D.H. (1989) *Preschool in Three Cultures: Japan, China and the United States* (New Haven: Yale University Press).

Trancik, A. & Evans, G. (1995) 'Spaces Fit for Children: Competency in the Design of Daycare Centre Environments' in *Children's Environments*, 12 (3), pp. 45–58.

Trevarthen, C. (1992) 'An Infant's Motives for Thinking and Speaking' in A.H. Wold (ed.) *Dialogical Alternatives* (Oxford: Oxford University Press).

Tuan, Y-F. (1974) *Topophilia: A Study of Environmental Perception, Attitudes, and Values* (Englewood Cliffs, New Jersey: Prentice-Hall Inc).

Tuan, Y-F. (1977) *Space and Place: The Perspective of Experience* (Minneapolis: University of Minnesota Press).

Tuan, Y-F. (1998) 'A Life of Learning', Charles Homer Haskins lecture for 1998, American Council of Learned Societies, Occasional Paper No. 42, retrieved November 2004 from http://www.acls.org/op42tuan.htm.

Tudge, J., Gray, J.T. & Hogan, D.M. (1997) 'Ecological Perspectives in Human Development: A Comparison of Gibson and Bronfenbrenner' in J. Tudge, M.J. Shanahan, & J. Valsiner (eds.) *Comparisons in Human Development: Understanding Time and Context* (Cambridge, Cambridge University Press), pp. 72–105.

United National Committee on the Rights of the Child, United Nations Children Fund and Bernard van Leer Foundation (2006) *A Guide to General Comment 7: Implementing Child Rights in Early Childhood* (The Hague: Bernard van Leer Foundation).

United Nations (1989) *United Nations Convention on the Rights of the Child*, Adopted by the UN General Assembly, 20 November 1989.

URBACT, EU (2007) URBACT, Integrated urban development transnational exchange, social inclusion in Europe, The Urbact Website, http:/urbact.eu/, accessed October 2007.

Valentine, G., & McKendrick, J. (1997) 'Children's Outdoor Play: Exploring Parental Concerns about Children's Safety and the Changing Nature of Childhood', *Geoforum*, 28, pp. 219–235.

Valsiner, J. (1997) *Culture and the Development of Children's Action: A Theory of Human Development* (NY: Wiley).

Valsiner, J. (1988) *Developmental Psychology in the Soviet Union* (Brighton: Harvester).

van Keulen, A. (2004) *Young Children Aren't Biased, Are They?!: How to Handle Diversity in Early Childhood Education and School* (Amsterdam: SWP).

van Liempd, I. & Hoekstra, E. (2007) *Van Visie Naar Ruimte: Handleiding voor Afstemming van Accommodaties in de Kinderopvang op de Pedagogische Visie* [From Pedagogical Vision to Use of Space: Guidelines for Relating the Design of Early Childhood Environments to Pedagogical Aims and Vision] (Waarborgfonds Kinderopvang/AKTA, onderzoeks-en adviesbureau voor ruimtegebruik).

Vecchi, V. (1998) 'What Kind of Space for Living Well in School?' in G. Ceppi & M. Zini (eds.) *Children, Spaces, Relations: Metaproject for an Environment for Young Children* (Reggio Emilia: Reggio Children and Comue di Reggio Emilia), pp. 128–135.

Vygotsky, L. (1978) *Mind in Society: The Development of Higher Psychological Processes* (Cambridge MA: Cambridge University Press).

Ward, C. (1978) *The Child in the City* (London: Architectural Press).

Warming, H. & Kampmann, J. (2007) 'Children in Command of Time and Space' in H. Zeiher, D. Devine, A. Kjørholt, H. Strandell (eds.)

Children's Times and Spaces: Changes in Welfare in an Intergenerational Perspective (Odense, University Press of Southern Denmark).

Warming, H. (2005) 'Participant Observation: A Way to Learn about Children's Perspectives' in A. Clarke, A.T. Kjørholt & P. Moss (eds.) *Beyond Listening: Children's Perspectives on Early Childhood Services* (Bristol: Policy Press), pp. 51–70.

Weikart, D.P. (ed.) (1999) *What Should Young Children Learn? Teacher and Parent Views in 15 Countries* (Ypsilanti, MI:High/Scope Press).

Weikart, D.P., Olmsted, P.P. & Montie, J. (2003). *World of Preschool Experience: Observation in 15 Countries* (Ypsilanti, MI: High/Scope Press).

Weiss, H. (2005) 'The Evaluation Exchange', Harvard Family Research Project, Harvard Graduate School of Education, Vol. XI, 4, winter 2005/06.

Wells, G. (1987) *The Meaning-Makers: Children Learning Language and Using Language to Learn* (London: Hodder & Stoughton).

Wertsch, J.V. (1991) *Voice of the Mind: A Sociocultural Approach to Mediated Action* (Cambridge, MA: Harvard University Press).

Wertsch, J.V. (1998) *Mind in Action* (Cambridge, MA: Harvard University Press).

Whitbread, N. (1972) *The Evolution of the Nursery-Infant School: A History of Infant and Nursery Education in Britain, 1800–1970* (London: Routledge & Kegan Paul).

Wilderspin, S. (1840) *A System for the Education of the Young* (London: James S. Hodson).

Winegar, L. & Valsiner, L. (eds.) (1992) *Children's Development within Social Context: Vol. 2, Research and Methodology* (Hillsdale NJ: Erlbaum).

Wollons, R. (2000) 'On the International Diffusion, Politics, and Transformation of the Kindergarten', Introduction in R. Wollons (ed.) *Kindergarten and Cultures* (New Haven: Yale University Press), pp. 1–15.

Wood, D. (1988) *How Children Think and Learn* (Oxford: Blackwell Publishers).

Wood, D., Bruner, J. & Ross, G. (1976) 'The Role of Tutoring in Problem-solving', *Journal of Child Psychology and Psychiatry*, 17, pp. 89–100.

Wood, E. (1999) 'The Impact of the National Curriculum on Play in Reception Classes', *Educational Research*, Vol. 41, pp. 11–22.

Woodhead, M. (2006) *Changing Perspectives on Early Childhood: Theory, Research and Policy* (UNESCO).

Woodhead, M. (1999) 'Towards a Global Paradigm for Research into Early Childhood Education', *European Early Childhood Education Research Journal*, Vol. 7, No. 1, pp. 5–22.

Woodhead, M. (1996) *In Search of the Rainbow: Pathways to Quality in Large-scale Programmes for Young Disadvantaged Children* (The Hague: Bernard van Leer Foundation).

Woodhead, M. Faulkner, D. & Littleton, K. (1998) *Cultural Worlds of Early Childhood* (London: Routledge in association with Open University).

Yolton, J.W. & Yolton J.S. (2000) *John Locke: Some Thoughts Concerning Education* (Oxford: Oxford Press).

Zeiher, H. (2003) 'Shaping Daily Life in Urban Environments' in P. Christensen & M. O'Brien (eds.) *Children in the City: Home, Neighbourhood and Community* (London: Routledge Falmer), pp. 66–81.

Zero To Three (1999) 'Response to The Myth of the First Three Years', retrieved 3 October 1999 http://www.zerotothree.org/no-myth.html.

Index